PERMANENT RECORD
POETICS TOWARDS THE ARCHIVE

PERMANENT RECORD
POETICS TOWARDS THE ARCHIVE

EDITED BY NAIMA YAEL TOKUNOW

NIGHTBOAT BOOKS

NEW YORK

Copyright © 2025 by Nightboat Books
Introduction and editing copyright © 2025 by Naima Yael Tokunow

All rights reserved
Printed in the United States

ISBN: 978-1-643-62242-2

Cover: "Pink Entrance" by Nika Milano. Reprinted with permission of the artist.

Design and typesetting by Kit Schluter
Typeset in Minion & AFRONAUT

Thanks to these rights holders for permission to reprint the following poems:

Rosa Alcalá, "You, Amateur Interpreter" and "You to the Future" from *YOU* (Coffee House Press, 2024). Copyright © 2024 by Rosa Alcalá. Reprinted with permission of Coffee House Press.

Lillian-Yvonne Bertram, "Doomsday" from *Negative Money*. Copyright © 2023 by Lillian-Yvonne Bertram. Reprinted with the permission of The Permissions Company, LLC on behalf of Soft Skull Press, an imprint of Counterpoint Press.

Mahogany L. Browne, "The 19th Amendment & My Mama." Copyright © 2020 by Mahogany L. Browne. Reprinted by the permission of The Charlotte Sheedy Literary Agency as agent for the author.

Ina Cariño, "It Feels Good to Cook Rice" and "bitter melon" from *Feast*. Copyright © 2023 by Ina Cariño. Reprinted with the permission of The Permissions Company, LLC on behalf of Alice James Books.

Brenda Shaughnessy, "Tell Our Mothers We Tell Ourselves the Story We Believe Is Ours" from *Tanya: Poems*. Copyright © 2023 by Brenda Shaughnessy. Used by permission of Alfred A. Knopf, an imprint of the Knopf Doubleday Publishing Group, a division of Penguin Random House LLC. All rights reserved.

Cataloging-in-publication data is available from the Library of Congress

Nightboat Books
New York
www.nightboat.org

TABLE OF CONTENTS

INTRODUCTION • *xi*

MOTHERTONGUED • 1

MELISA CASUMBAL-SALAZAR
FILIPINO V. FILIPINX • 3
ST. MARY'S ACADEMY FOR ASPHYXIATION BY VANILLA • 5
DESCENDANTS' DALIT • 10

CAROLINA EBEID
from WINTERNET • 14

CARI MUÑOZ
NOTHING MORE THAN PHONETIC COINCIDENCES • 18

ROSA ALCALÁ
YOU, AMATEUR INTERPRETER • 19

KATHY WU
THE SEA BLACK AND BOILING • 20

INA CARIÑO
BITTER MELON • 21

JADE CHO
萍 • 23

EM DIAL
NECROPASTORAL IN THE CANYON OF THE WOMB • 24
QUADROON (ADJ., N.) • 25

LUCIAN MATTISON
MARK/SIGN • 27

MORIANA DELGADO
NOUN-ME, WOULD YOU? • 29

<u>FILE NOT FOUND</u> • 31

KATHARINA LUDWIG
THE COLLECTION OF UN-HEALING • 33

JALYNN HARRIS
I'LL KILL HIM MY OWN GAHTDAMN SELF! • 37

JACLYN DESFORGES
FLOWER GIRL • 38

MAKSHYA TOLBERT
TREE WALK WITH WORRY • 39

LILLIAN-YVONNE BERTRAM
DOOMSDAY GRID • 40

CHAUN WEBSTER
from WITHOUT TERMINUS • 42

GABRIEL RIDOUT
SPAM EATER • 52

SJ KIM-RYU
NATURALLY NO • 53

MAX GREGG
HOMOSEXUALITY ("CURES") • 54

BRENDA SHAUGHNESSY
TELL OUR MOTHERS WE TELL OURSELVES
THE STORY WE BELIEVE IS OURS • 56

SAFIA ELHILLO
THE ROOM • 64

MAHOGANY L. BROWNE
THE 19TH AMENDMENT & MY MAMA • 66

STEFANIA GOMEZ
THE KEEPER • 69

KATHY WU
WERNER'S NOMENCLATURE OF • 74

LORRAINE RICE
OF BEING WILL & TESTAMENT • 75
FAMILY HISTORY IN ABSTRACT • 77

THE MAP AS MISDIRECTION • 83

LILLIE WALSH
ACCORDED A NEW RECOLLECTION • 85

ESTHER G. BELIN
REVOLT OF THE RE-TERRITORIALIZED TONGUE • 91

SASHA BURSHTEYN
LAMINATION • 95
PANORAMA OF LIGHT • 96

HAZEM FAHMY
THE BILLIONAIRE • 100

ABIGAIL SWOBODA
IN BULK • 102
DOVER TASTES WORSE THAN DALLASTOWN • 103

PAUL S UKRAINETS
PERSPECTIVE GRID • 104

EMILY HOLLANDER
THE SCIENCE PODCAST BROS TELL ME WHAT LIFE IS • 106

DAVID GREENSPAN
from GLITCH, MICHIGAN • 107

PALOMA YANNAKAKIS
RUNOFF ZONE • 111

FUTURE CONTINUOUS • 117

TALIA FOX
NOTES ON TIME TRAVEL IN THE MATRILINEAL LINE • 119

INA CARIÑO
IT FEELS GOOD TO COOK RICE • 121

ROSA ALCALÁ
YOU TO THE FUTURE • 124

GERAMEE HENSLEY
DEARLY BELOVED (A PREFATORY QUADRAPHONICS) • 125

DOUGLAS KEARNEY
TEEF • 126

MYLO LAM
TRI NHAN 004 WITNESSES & SONNETIZES
A STARLING MURMURATION • 134

GERÓNIMO SARMIENTO CRUZ
from WHALEFALL • 135

LORRAINE RICE
AFFIDAVIT OF LOSS • 142

P.C. VERRONE
ARC-HIVE • 144

JAN-HENRY GRAY
ENCORE & ON A LOOP • 145
ON THERAPY • 146

LENA KASSICIEH
AYAM ZAMAN • 147

CONTRIBUTOR BIOS • 151

EDITOR BIO • 156

ACKNOWLEDGMENTS • 157

INTRODUCTION

Archives of/Against Absence: exploring identity, collective memory, and the unseen

> *if you are not a myth, whose reality are you? If you are not a reality, whose myth are you?*
>
> —SUN RA, *Prophetika*, Book One

> *I will have spent my life trying to understand the function of remembering, which is not the opposite of forgetting, but rather its lining. We do not remember. We rewrite memory much as history is rewritten. How can one remember thirst?*
>
> —CHRIS MARKER, *Sans Soleil*

AN INVITATION: *I am writing this introduction in a coffee shop on the corner of Mountain Road and Forrester Avenue on unceded Tewa land, known as Albuquerque, New Mexico, with a little sweat on my lip, my tongue slightly burned, sitting with all the pasts of all the worlds of the poems in this book. I am brought to Kara Walker's question on memory, "whether or not there is such a thing as a past and a present, or if the present is just like the past with new clothes on."*[1] *I look at the clothes of this book and their threads and think of your hands, the ways in which we can see ourselves in each other's seams. The photographer Naima Green (no relation, only reflection) asks, "What pieces of the present are missing from the archives of the future?"*[2] *The record welcomes.*

You are now a part of the record of this book. Write your name in it. Your name, now in the book, is a part of the book and a part of the book's remembering. This is not an exercise, not metaphor. The cells of your fingers, your breath, meet the page. This collection is only complete now, with the work, its frame, and you, all pressed against each other—your witnessing, our words. We mark the book, thumb through pages. The book marks us, both in the now.

---

1. Harvey, Matthea. "Kara Walker." *BOMB Magazine*, July 1, 2007.
2. Othering & Belonging Institute. "Naima Green | Interview." Cultures of Care, University of California, Berkeley.

xi

Before coming to this project, I had spent nearly a decade thinking critically about the Black American record (or lack thereof), and how my understanding of myself as a Black American, my family, and my culture has been shaped by what I can, and do, know through searching archives. These archives include materials from my family and the state, from papers and oral histories, and from political and artistic recordings. Many records are missing, misremembered, or unfindable. Some are full and jumbled, hard to decipher. Most are couched in death, grief, and loss. This cannot be and is not the "full story," although we are socialized to understand records as such, rewarded for reinforcing its "wholeness," and often penalized for pointing to its deficiencies. Many have written beautifully about the wound of not-knowing—our homeland, our people, our tongues, our separation from culture.[3]

I am also a first-generation "Israeli" American. I would not exist without the Zionist, violent project of Israel. As settler colonial states often do, the state of Israel took existing records of Palestinian life—of land, of home, of history—and erased them by destroying libraries, religious archives, whole communities, and whatever didn't serve its mission, rewriting history to bolster its own false narratives. The current genocide in Gaza is the most recent and brutal product of this ongoing erasure.

And so, I am drawn to this question of healing the archive in part to deepen my relationships to the ancestors and family I have lost, and who have been made lost to me I wonder, how might our work of prefiguring the archives of the future prevent further erasure?

A book whose spark started with my positionality and interests in the archive bloomed into something more than what I know, feel, or could hold. An opportunity for us, as thinkers and makers and writers, as poets, to both name the harms of these rotten records and seed with an eye toward future abundance in how and who and where we understand our very being(s).

* * *

As I created the framework for this anthology, thinking broadly about the epistemology of dominant culture and canon—I wondered, what damage had

---

3. I think of the following writers and thinkers exploring the holes, obfuscations, and gaps in the archive: Fred Moten, Frantz Fanon, Katherine McKittrick, Patricia J. Williams, John L. Jackson Jr, Toni Morrison, James Baldwin, and, and, and (the book, in fact, could just be a list like this).

the archive done to our ability to hold ancestral knowledge and pass it to our children? Our own stories? The archive here is conceptualized as the commodification (and weaponization) of a shared cultural recording. It includes, but is not limited to: the canon, written record, and other "legitimate" ways of knowing and forms of documenting.

And so, *Permanent Record* hopes to apply the kind of pressure that turns matter from one thing to another by asking hard questions: How do we reject, interpolate, and (re)create the archive and record? How do we feed our fragmented recordings to health? How do we pull blood from stone (and ink and shadows and ghosts)? What do we gain from our flawed systems of remembrance? How does creating a deep relationship to the archive allows us both agency and legibility, allow us to prefigure the world we want? Through this reclamation, we can become the ancestors we didn't have.

Permanent Record wants to reimagine who is included in the archive and which recordings are considered worthy of preservation, making room for the ways many of us have had to invent forms of knowing in and from delegitimatized spaces and records. In doing so, we explore "possibilities for speculating beyond recorded multiplicity" (thank you, Trisha Low, for this perfect wording). This book itself is a record. The book asks what can be counted as an epistemological object. What is counted. Who is counted, and how.

* * *

While designing the call for this book, I named frameworks for our poets to respond to. Throughout, contributors play with collage, the space of the page, and image, experimenting with forms both familiar and new—to reimagine the page of the archive is to make it our own, or something else entirely. And in these ways, both in content and form, the book grapples with, teases out, lambasts, and otherwise yokes itself to the archive as a network of mycelium, interdependent and growing just below the surface.

In "Mothertongued," I asked for responses and reflections on identity and language, diasporic and first-generation lived experiences, fluency, multilingual and monolingual explorations, inquiries into words and their (de)colonial work, and the codes/keys of the archive. For Kathy Wu in "The Sea Black and Boiling,"

> Language membranes — a nuance — from conquering / eyes — Lapis Lazuli — theirs is a zoological love — Grape / Hyacinth — it is nape and pin — it is Upper Side of the Wings of / Small Heath Butterfly — the hour of science...

The poem layers language, cuts of color, the moth wing and mouse throat, all against the backdrop of a sea, its language both undulating and inertial, washing over the reader. Lucian Mattison turns to the roots of the English alphabet in "Mark/Sign:"

> Revolution hears with more than ears, fights the unnamed everything
> with a broad-nib reed pen
> in wet clay..."

We addressed the holes in the archive in "File Not Found," asking: where does our unknowing lead us? How do we create our own records, borrow from others, and construct narratives that aren't fictional yet aren't based on "known fact?" What tensions arise there (e.g., who's missing, what's missing, where are the redactions and omissions)? Safia Elhillo answers with literal holes in space—"What bothers me today is that I cannot remember. In the Zamalek / apartment, in Cairo, I remember / all the rooms but one…"—while Jaclyn Desforges reminds us that "Your father is a series of photocopied fathers," pointing to what is lost in our renderings and rememberings.

"The Map as Misdirection" examines both the archive of the colonial nation-state, the ways that the record upholds harm and provides incomplete understandings, and the way that we organize and chart our records. In "Lamination," Sasha Burshteyn creates an alternative chart of present Ukraine—

> "Steppe // city // lake // lake // biosphere // desert // canyon // become metaphors for the nation. Nation = waterfall. Nation = granite

—refusing the way present-day imperial violence demands nation-states and borders. "This is where memory will be held, performed, and instructed. In order to map the ways in which memory is housed and tucked away for later use a cast of objects will appear here." Lillie Walsh demystifies the work of archival accessioning, how we literally map our histories.

The poems in "Future Continuous" share dreams, hopes, and fears about how we are ma(r)king the future today. How and what are we leaving as records for our future(s)? What kind of future is being built in the now through the way we record? What will we leave for our descendants to use as records to build their own epistemologies? Gerónimo Sarmiento Cruz asks us to mold our own figures towards some other shores in the selection from "Whalefall"—"you choose your face / &prerogative / we'll craft the mask / &head seaward," while Lorraine Rice pledges her allegiance to the ancestors: "I, daughter of havoc, having been duly sworn to collect and keep the memories in accordance with ghosts."

Each section begins with an introduction of sorts—a lyric map legend to the work within, inviting you to pull the threads of the framework through the pieces. I hope this book moves you, as it has me, towards some new edge, an opening in the possibility of record, document, and the archive of traceable memory. As Octavia E. Butler reminds us, "There is nothing new under the sun, but there are new suns." This book hopes to contribute to the maps that will lead us to those new solar systems, ones where we can heal and be free.

NAIMA YAEL TOKUNOW

ALBUQUERQUE, NEW MEXICO

PERMANENT RECORD

POETICS TOWARDS THE ARCHIVE

MOTHERTONGUED

Our language known, our language underwater. Here are our people, their hands like mirrors and oceans. We are the first and the fiftieth mouth to hold these sounds. The trick of speech and character, the treat of the syllable disoriented. Word-fucked and proper nouned. The words that endure, written on the ephemeral. Who gets to interpret and who remains untranslatable? Here, tongues both knotted and snaking.

MELISA CASUMBAL-SALAZAR

FILIPINO V. FILIPINX

Can *diaspora born Filipinx* be anything but tautological. Do you familiar scent dog-invoking slurs. I dog. I abhor & adore actually the dogfights. I fanatically observe all dogs but blood sport drowses, disorients. Why must we Be like that. All doggings are mine; I repose deep eternally every dog. That is when I am.

In the avid, anecdotal observation of identitarian claim-making by Fils: ferocity. In diaspora. In the Philippines. Swimming fiber optic cable. We dogged wherever & all time we dig. We thus resist declaims to authenticate, homogenize, yet irresistible still we claim. Authenticity as declaration as regulative ideal: Here Dog, This Dog. Heel. Pure. Treat.

The provocation of *Filipinx & Pilipinx*: enactment, utterance, interpellation. Do you howl the alphas the cower diaspora. Tao is only Tagalog for people. Gender-neuter Filipino paddle over eighty languages & archipelago. Who declares dialects yours. Dialects language which. Fixed language fixes print border. What does swimming language sink.

When true value *Filipina* true *Filipino* constitutes dog universal. Compass gender Filipina. Genealogy anti-linear language sport best in show movement. Tao ☙ Tao in 80+ languages ☙ Infièle ☙ Indio ☙ Mestizo ☙ Mestiza Tribus Independientes ☙ Moro ☙ Indios Bravas ☙ Illustrado ☙ Native Malay ☙ Philippine ☙ Native ☙ Filipino ☙ Filipina ☙ Comfort Woman Pinoy ☙ Little Brown Brother ☙ Philippine Citizen ☙ Dogeater

Filipino-American/Fil-Am ⋅૭ Flip ⋅૭ Pinay ⋅૭ Pilipino ⋅૭ Pilipina Filipino Filipino/ Fil-Fil ⋅૭ U.S.-born Filipino/Filipina ⋅૭ Forgotten Asian Americans ⋅૭ little brown fucking machine powered by rice military base shop t-shirt tagline ⋅૭ Filipin@ ⋅૭ Pinayism ⋅૭ Blacks of Asia ⋅૭ Filipina/o/x ⋅૭ Decolonial Pin@y

Why must we Chase the cat. Flash glinty canines.

Howl. Dog. Swim.

ST. MARY'S ACADEMY FOR ASPHYXIATION BY VANILLA

For you, Nanay,

Papa ceased reading mahjong tiles with his fingertips.
For Papa, his parents & kapatid, there was no U.S. Navy sail to citizen.
There was you.

Petition after Petition for Alien Relatives, five hundred dollars a pop.

As routine as rice.

Titas, titos, cousins, weeks & months moored, knotted to launch from the
    guest room.
Playmates & punchline archives. Nannies, dentist, accountant, architect, chef.
A tack from tago ng tago to wed to fists.

I loaned her money for the abortion.

Cite the skin & stubble

her clavicle heels reiterate the fit of our material angles.
Hips in the timbre & cleave in the key of
pinay binabae bakla tibo anak.

Every ideal regulated for diurnal & lunar performance.

Dead star crisp ceilings 1986 Annandale VA.

Your sampaguita duster & gray hairs akimbo, forty-six years' resolute.
Like you'd never loved wrong.
On loop again, *What's wrong with you, ha?! So selfish! So stupid!*

I drain into a Bad Brains t-shirt, eat shame.

They ran the stop.

Maroon station wagon of self-rule. That breakup white boy.
What white couple's Absolut keeling. Your accordioned Civic.
The bloodless boy lopes home. I curb alone, observe thigh swell & police.

Not your fault but *Big dude driver. Not legally drunk.*
How you hid the ore of your sinking til you reared, tsunami.

Papa's aquiline, burgis parents. The pierce of their knowing
their son's deservingness. Better than our pamilya's petit bourgeois.
Better than your baby daddy opera.

Plenitude of my un-placeability.

It's a nice apartment building, all seniors.

Gasping eyebrows in-law. Papa's dropped chin of disgrace.
To scorn you then expect your perpetual care, your complete repertoire of
    tenderness,
your coin, & Papa at the bowling alley.

They've never even offered me a cold glass of water.

The eviscerating conviction of your hiss.

God punished you. My cheeks puddled silent.
You twisted. *You weren't like this before.*
Come back to Church.

Nope.

Who were the you who pronounced, *No sex until marriage, ha! You won't want
 to stop if you start.*

Reiterate, cite the body's mattering. The packer & bind, the family fiesta face.
I cited Mbwende's shave gait & Sinead. You cite Nora Aunor, Maria Clara.
Iteration kinks the space time makes.

Everything I do is for my family.

In 1953, before your father bloodied you, you longed to be a nun.

I try & try to cite you, piano at the nursing home, choir flute.
Your white church lady friends coo at my pious bastard dog show paces.
Christened & confirmed I dematerialize.

What is wrong with you, ha?! Why are you like this?!

St. Mary's Academy for Asphyxiation by Vanilla

You are vexed & defend. *It's a good school. Expensive!* Why does good mean
 1 Filipino,
1 Korean, 1 Vietnamese, 1 Salvadoran, 1 Black girl? White girls of course
 feign care

7

then mock & destroy, but the newly arrived girl from Hong Kong, too?

Why am I like what, Nanay? Anarcho-effigist? Bi-licious? Femme-querying? Peminist?

You keened & lunged to beat me.

I'm never going to mass again.
Your hands remember my shoulders squaring to shovel you away,
irises flashing the unimaginable.

Breaths next, you disclosed the truth about my father.

What is wrong with you, ha?! Why are you like this?!

Like what? Mutinous? Starved for volition?
Avalanched in rage? Allured by manifestos of transcendence, transformation, rebirth?
Do you recall Tito Romy's mic drop?

Do you mean, *just like you*?

In the community to come, citation will be wild & free.

A riverine girl, you climbed a stool, twitched the Santa Mesa tap.
The water's clarity & rush thrilled you. Your Nanay swooped, dammed the flow,
slapped & pinched you into knowing its precious expense.

In the community to come, you are a nun & painter who lives by a stream.

Buffeted, we both, between spot lit & undetectable in doctrinal diaspora.

You resist too, Nanay. Shall we rename the grip? If not patriarchies,
brown & white, then power's calcification? If not class hierarchy, then cruel expectations?
If not raced gender, then stripped autonomy, stalled community?

In percussion & pileups we forget what we share: how to howl, when to dog, what to swim.

DESCENDANTS' DALIT

a dalit is a meditative verse form, sometimes written in eight-syllable quatrains, originally intended to offer catholic or spanish-language instruction. ° inay • *mother* ° puede ba • with attitude, as in *girl, please, for real?* ° buntis • *pregnant* ° kawayan • *bamboo* • in tagalog creation stories, Maganda, the first woman, is freed from a bamboo stem by a *kite* or *raptor*. ° ama • *father* ° bakla • *reappropriated slur for gay or feminine man* ° amihan • *cool season of the northeast wind, follows monsoon season* ° tibo • *reappropriated slur for lesbian or masculine woman* ° binhi • *seed* ° clutch heads leaking against her ribs • although now most associated with the Cordillera, head-taking was historically practiced throughout the philippines as an aspect of traditional governance & war. its elimination was a priority under spanish & american colonialism. ° barkada • *crew, best friends, fam* ° epz • *export processing zone* ° lolas • *grandmothers* ° sawsawan • *special sauce* ° pasyon • passion play depicting the life & death of christ, performed ritually during holy week. in *Pasyon & Revolution*, historian Reynaldo Ileto describes the pasyon as an epic form that, while introduced by the spanish for colonial pacification, had the unintended effect of providing christianized filipinos with a semiotics of anti-colonial liberation. ° harana • *serenade* ° dreamoir • see Wendy C. Ortiz, *Bruja* ° we cacerolazo siren woks & pots • a sonic modality of solidarity & community recognition of the perpetration of intimate partner violence; practiced primarily by women. ° balimbing • *traitor*

your line's enduring:
fist moist priest palms
stone against our tracheas
& labias contused.

you light scorch for yourself
sneak contempt for inay
hid spleen curve deep
tendering generations

tonguing grief heat like
a newborn Palawan peacock.
& whose namesake
sheens the enduring?

& how much buried treason?
cease please your squall for
this thrill krait of
no consequence

this krilling motherless
no-account roach
cast out by the
Crocodile Queens who

waste no good salty water.
puede ba!
because he abandoned your
buntis belly for another

giggled your earlobe
tender in his teeth
til your lungs filled his jaw,
til he panted your breath?

although
with the   & so we soar from   *now most associated*
ing was   acacia to acacia   *Cordillera, head-tak-*
through-   until we are spent   *historically practiced*
as an aspect of tradi-   waiting, intoning for   *out the philippines*
governance & war.   the temple of your belly   *tional*
elimination was a   to be self-disgust-   *its*
under spanish &   free & crowded   *priority*
can colonialism.   with conjure.   *ameri-*
ada • crew, best   *° bark-*
fam ° epz •   your inay cleft kawayan.   *friends,*
processing zone   her ama , a tributary.   *export*
grandmothers °   their bakla, the amihan.   *° lolas •*
    our tibo binhi clutch heads   *sawsawan*
•   leaking against her ribs.   *special sauce °*
pasyon   her barkada unravel the mobius of   *• passion*
play   sugar & mangasm capital   *depicting the*
life &   santa galleons & epz lie-pounding.   *death of christ,*
performed   *ritually*
during holy   the lolas, the paddlers   *week. in*
Pasyon &   preserve the line sawsawan.   *Revolution,*
historian   time now to shrimp paste   *Reynaldo*
    our salty water pasyon
Ileto describes the
pasyon to harana limbs akimbo   *pasyon as an epic form*
to complect your dreamoir   *that, while introduced by*
to dessicate.   *the spanish for colonial*
pasyon for the sighing.
pacifica-   *tion, had*
the unin-   we cacerolazo woks & pots,   *tended*
effect of   lamentation for the neighbor's breaking.   *providing*
    her clocked beating stops.
    we cantileve.

unfit to taste your name
the balimbing you wail to forget
whose world bathed you in shame
his treachery is our machete

don't you see the felled
season now to swoon the
abyssal currents. spearfish
our archive of misfeeling

CAROLINA EBEID

from WINTERNET

(where do the ancestors gather?) — Brandon Shimoda

Dear Brandon,

My son Patrick and I were at my computer typing words into google translate, from english to arabic. It's a femme, computure-generated voice that speaks the arabic words, and when you press the "listen" button a second time, she speaks the words very slowly. The word for water, rose, war, sea, pillow, sky… then I transliterated these sounds into my notebook.

Then something happened, a glitch!

When we refreshed the page, every previous pronouncement, every slow enunciation played for 10 seconds of simultaneous talking.

We refreshed a second time and it happened again / a sudden market place of voices.

I opened my phone's voice memo app and recorded it. I attach it here.

Perhaps the ancestors are in the dna (and how it travels), in language (and how language travels). And (what about) in glitches? Are they there? Can we say they find a slit or tear in the digital universe to speak through to us?

I need courage. Do you have any to send my way?

Caro,

I think all the courage is theirs . . .
The women, their voices, in the marketplace . . .

And in the permission they're giving . . .

What were their voices before you and Patrick created the glitch?

Or . . . where?

You refreshed the page! That is what happened: you refreshed the page . . .

The page has been refreshed. And now the marketplace comes to life . . .

The video poem has already been made. Maybe it just needs another glitch to be created . . .

Or the page to be refreshed again . . .

Glitch: a sudden surge of current . . .

Brandon

[written on hide]

*

—of animals, softened by soaking, tanned, toughened,
stretched over a hollow cylinder to make a drum

—of concealment, what is hidden under the shirt
hide and seek, run and hide for survival, for play

*

If you grew out of your (winter,
thought, purse, chest cavity)
would I, I would be plant-wise
wiser for the spiny-edge & milk
veins, this wonder's so ancient
so Mesopotamian, look at Miriam
who covers her mouth when she
laughs, look at Miriam who wears
her dress like a casket

You have to use the telepathy machine: feelings as artifacts
You have to use a channel (O) for an ancestor to pass through
Yawn her up from the white space, in alphanumeric names
their cambered arabic numerals, a semetic pneumatic, a numen

*

emerge (transitive., imp.):   emerge the _____ out of the _____

information	miracle	sleep
sound	burning car	throat
child	music	possibility

*

Hippocamus controls short & long memory, named *horse + sea-monster* or *seahorse* for its shape, though the man who described the anatomy first called it a *silkworm*, then changed his mind. The silkworm eats of the mullberry leaves. From holes in its jaws, the silkworm excretes thread in circular movements, wirl-a-world, self-cocooning. In this video, the brain lights up where a new memory forms.

CARI MUÑOZ

NOTHING MORE THAN
PHONETIC COINCIDENCES

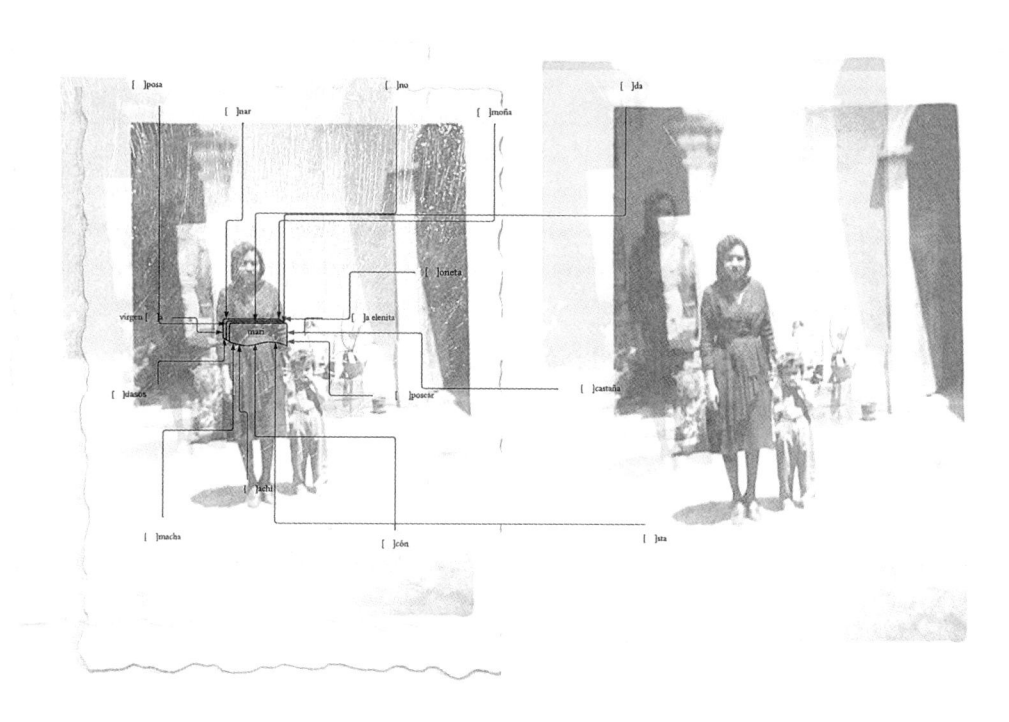

ROSA ALCALÁ

YOU, AMATEUR INTERPRETER

You would have told yourself as your mother sat in the dentist's chair, had you known who Wittgenstein was then, "I have to imagine pain which I do not feel on the model of the pain which I do feel." You would have considered whether deep nerve pain was more akin to an arm scraping against pavement or to the head struck by a slipper flung from across a room just after breakfast. But that wouldn't have solved the problem of translation: first, build the model, then describe its components in another language so that the model falls apart and becomes another. Meaning, could you have described your mother's pain to the doctor in English, even if you felt it in your own jaw? You'd watched your Mamá's teeth being pulled or a mold made of her mouth. Dentures have to fit perfectly, or they hurt. You did your best, telling her to bite down hard into the wax. Did your parents ever have a full set of teeth? When you had yours pulled—the wisdom and the one dead at the root—there was nothing to interpret but the ether. So you lay back in leather and let the dentist, like a lover, blow smoke into your mouth until the chair began to swirl—a tipsy teacup at the church bazaar—and whip your hair around. Later, you got a well-paid gig at Avon's international awards dinner and sat with the top Latin American sellers, and, oh god, you were hungry and didn't have half the words for the cosmetic industry. But the agency never bothered to ask, so you faked it and brought home leftovers. Those ladies deserved better than your parent-teacher conference training. Anyone in the kitchen could have done a better job. In high school, when you tried to test out of Spanish and were asked to spell out numbers, you thought, qué fácil, but ended up in the same group as the metal chicks from the suburbs. When you were a baby, Papá's first English swung into the back of the restaurant with each stack of dishes, and with a box of diapers under each arm, he'd come home singing, "Happy Birthday, para mí. Happy Birthday, para mí."

THE SEA BLACK AND BOILING

in Mandarin, 清 evershifts — tensing jade, sky blue, indigo, no — a clear spring, cognate to living — evasion, invasion. In Congolese Ndembu, a negated area greens — water rinsed in sweet potato leaf, allowing. Language membranes — a nuance — from conquering eyes — Lapis Lazuli — theirs is a zoological love — Grape Hyacinth — it is nape and pin — it is Upper Side of the Wings of Small Heath Butterfly — the hour of science — Flax Flower — Light Parts of the Margin — these wordthings — Ultramarine — of the Wings of Devil's Butterfly — Feathers of Jay — of the sweet unconquered quay — Verditter — in lenticular — Sapphire — Ore, or Greenish — Turquois. Flour Spar — untarred, asserting slippage — Iron Earth — The Throat of it, didn't this used to be sea — here in pigmented blissing — the cast of light — casts a forensic you — a fabled igneous you — the color of — Fennel Flower — geologic unsoured, humble me — into stone. it is sargasso undulating — mountain ever contouring — Throat of Blue Titmouse — these are the stakes. Leave before you are — found Stamina of Single Purple Anemone — this is enduring, Breast of Emerald crested Manakin — this is not elegy, your-knot-knowing — your Copper Ore — Scotch — China Blue — Rhynchites Nitens — Back Parts of Gentian Flowers — so surely Azure —

INA CARIÑO

BITTER MELON

balsam pear. wrinkled gourd.
        leafy thing raised from seed.

pungent goya, ampalaya: cut
        & salt at the sink. spoon pulp

from bumpy rind, brown half-moons
        in garlic & sparking mantika.

like your nanay did. like your lola did.
        like your manang braving hot parsyak—

you'll wince. you'll think of the taste
        of your own green body—mapait

ang lasa. your sneer. masakit, dugo't
        laman. it hurts, this smack of bitter.

yes you'll remember how much it hurts,
        to nick your thumb as you bloom heat

in acid, sili at sukang puti—to grow up
        glowering in half-light—to flesh out

& plod through your own grassy way,
        unfurl your own crush of vines.

after you tip it onto a mound
        of steamed rice, as you chew,

the barb of it will hit the back
        of your throat. look at yourself,

square. you used to snarl at moths,
        start small blazes in entryways.

woodchip fires, flaking paint.
        look, tingnan mo—see your lip

curling in the glint of your bowl.
        unruly squash. acrid vegetable,

you'll flinch. you'll want to see
        nothing, taste like nothing. but

when you disappear your meal—
        when you choke on the last

chunky morsel of rice—you'll slurp
        thirsty for more—a saccharine life.

huwag mo akong kalimutan,
        you'll plead—

taste me.
taste me.

JADE CHO

萍

Ye Ye named his granddaughters 麗萍, 玉萍, 金萍: three types of duckweed. It is said he imagined a pond, the floating leaves shimmering at sunset. How to understand what you have not seen; I always thought the name unglamorous. Duckweed conjures scum on the surface of my childhood best friend's pool and the park pond too algaed to dip our feet in. An auntie tells me it is a common name for country girls from Hoisan. My mother talks often about our country shame: the Chinese visitor in her workplace who snickers that Szeyup is not real Cantonese. The cashier who giggles at her twang. My shame was not understanding my grandparents' language. I shrugged and squirmed when they spoke to me, hid in other rooms until they were dead. 萍 is the root of many Chinese metaphors: 萍蹤 tracks of a wanderer; 萍蹤靡定 travel with no fixed abode. In Beijing, a new friend calls me 小萍 as we stroll through afternoon haze. For the first time, my name becomes a dwelling. 萍 floats without roots.

NECROPASTORAL IN THE CANYON OF THE WOMB

TURN BACK TURN BACK TURN BACK
OUT OF CLAUSE BACK OUT OF THE CAUSE
AND EFFECT IS A LIE CAUSE AND AFFECT IS A LIE
DOWN AND PRETEND NOT TO SEE SCIENCE'S FACE FACE
SCIENCE AND SPIT THE WAY HE LIKES IT SIT LEGS SIDEWAYS
ACROSS THE HORSE'S BACK TO TRICK THEM THE STRAW BROKE
THE LEVEE AND HERE COMES THE FLOOD OF GLACIER CARVING
OVER GENERATIONS A GATE TO FREEDOM A GATED FREEDOM NO
PEARLS IN SIGHT INSIDE YOU AN OYSTER INSIDE THAT A KINGDOM
A KING DEMANDING SOME VERSION OF EROSION YOU ARE STOOD
AT THE EDGE YOU UNDERSTAND THE STAKES YOU MISTOOK YOU
FOR A LANDSLIDE A TRANSITION OF GRAVITY ALREADY SET IN
MOTION WIDENING LIKE A SHARK'S JAWS SO MUCH FURTHER
THAN YOU'D THINK POSSIBLE YOU ARE POSSIBLE AND
WERE WOMBED IN ORDER TO BE HERE AND AREN'T
RESPONSIBLE FOR THE FUTURE'S DROUGHT OR RAIN

QUADROON (ADJ., N.)

QUADROON (adj., n.); use it in a sentence: my mother teaches me about the "Four Corners" located in "the United States of America" and i imagine myself on all fours, like a mule braying to four audiences, each sees half a rump or face. a man can draw a crucifix over near anything and call it anything but a border. in this case, my fingers trace the cross-hairs of outlining the brightly colored squares on the map, and place my name and a pair of my ancestors in each of the quadrants.

QUADROON (adj., n.), *sounds like*: doubloon (see also: currencies), bassoon (see also: instruments), spittoon (see also: vessels for ejaculate), monsoon (see also: water), typhoon (see also: more than was allotted for), lagoon (see also: water), teaspoon (see also: only a little, by most standards), lampoon (see also: weapons), harpoon (see also: weapons), commune (see also: homes for many), cocoon (see also: a home for one), maroon (see also: the chestnut tree, or to leave stranded)

QUADROON (adj., n.) *language of origin*: once again, linguists spit their bloodied air: from Spanish *cuarteron*, or *one who has a fourth*. i pinch the linguist's tongues and gawk at the way they betray themselves. not *one who has three fourths*. not *the haystack with a needle inside*. instead, any drops of life in a sterile lake are isolated and named. the lake's volume is doubled again and again and again and again until science feels faultless renaming them Statistically Insignificant.

- - - - -

QUADROON (adj., n.), *definition*: could be a mule bound and quartered or the history of modern science. cracked like an egg, we arrive at: *quad*, as in, a way of dividing a globe into four, by way of a scalpel drawn across rainforest; and ruin, as in, a site of betrayal. *alternate definition*: a woman who cannot be trusted, or a woman whose womb was sold to whiteness, or a real woman who went to a mythic ball and never came home, or a woman, or a weapon, or a woman, or a weapon, or a woman, or

LUCIAN MATTISON

AUTHOR'S NOTE:

This is an excerpt from Root / Rudiment: An Abecedary, *which plays with the Levantine origins of our modern alphabet. Many of the Semitic letter names refer to concrete things and the letter shapes sometimes show similarities with their referents. This poem was written for the letter T.*

MARK/SIGN

Taw : T : +

Metal type weighs in the palm, maternal bricks
of water and snake, *mem* and *nun*. Revolution
hears with more than ears, fights the unnamed
everything with a broad-nib reed pen
in wet clay. A chisel to grey matter—allography
to typology, irreversible—consciousness is clipped
to the tympan, rolls along a berth of metal slugs
until plucked from the drum.
We can hardly keep up. Hundreds of thousands
of years of knowledge pushed into ceramic
pots, figures ligatured into root balls.
The corncob dwarfs its mummified ancestor,
treachery of artificial selection this Greek gift—
mark of modern language the dry rattle
of a walnut loose in its shell—image made sound,
a death knell. We tell the river reeds
they prefer to be plucked, used as styli.
A doorway was a doorway before its name,
and is now limited. Marks made

by an angled downstroke, the most
comfortable manner to hold an implement
decides twenty or so odd things, a number
well below our limits, and the last one leaves
its meaning on us like a bruise, every way
we can point outside of ourselves, use names
to separate us from the nature we are.

NOUN-ME, WOULD YOU?

You misgender my tongue and I like that. How awkward you look running when only the ventilator knows how to dance. So dance my glass on cough arrhythmic, letters were meant to look like animals hanging, unlike me, un-pure instinct, ill-fitting jacket, water-rash hyphenating what you speak not becoming. I am the same as making it happen. I know nothing about you: earbuds refuse to listen, the voice of fruit trapped always in your pocket, size not living up to the arbitrary arrangement of stars; so put it away, where I can see it, and hiss decompression, and powder into a mass of bony lagoon in plural tense; put it up front, vacuum my foreskin or blindfold me into light, walk with me inside the river, without skidding, walk into me now even if my time is only coffee time, no room for moon-cream, or in-complete dark, ness of what's less, the way herrings are present: continuous is this night of in-carnation splattered for dinner. But you're not dancing: your name is not supposed to be here. Your name of liquid burial. Your name that crushes cardamom but not enough. Your name that questions resemblance. Your name that nouns me. So time-me, would you? These are my new words: I miled the pound I owned ounce. So dance. Say I tried an olive-drab chest, and now it doesn't match the city, light resurrects me everywhere and forever from us-becoming, undisturbed laundry engulfing my ears, so dance and craft my world I time at times —

                        how far I stand from you,

                        aware of something

                        that's not aging.

FILE NOT FOUND

Record as mimesis, as memisis, a smemeesiss. Every step a hole, some mulch-filled, some barren. Where do we go when we go searching for the blood-filled answers? We dig in the trash, fingers cording like wall phones—back to the receiver, we are stretched to the limits of our imaginations. Our memories skip, hold out. We become the keepers, the last thread of the last stitch. We line up the fragments, work sweat to make them legible (mirror scraps), illegible (the code of secret messages). Sometimes the hole is just a hole and not a metaphor—stick your head down, a finger or other appendage. We remember creation was a myth pulled out of nothing. We pull.

KATHARINA LUDWIG

THE COLLECTION OF UN-HEALING

It will prove nearly impossible to speak about the Collection of Un-healing, as it will be constructed around and (from) within the unsayable. This doesn't mean it will be insignificant or expressionless even, its vacant appearances will not represent the emptiness of lack.

The Collection of Un-healing will consist of a conglomerate of numerous assembled structures that emerge/spring/open up all over the world. There will not be a headquarter, but rather a multiplicity of allied venues. Ancient and modern in appearance, the collection will defy style and genre as much as temporality itself. The Collection of Un-healing will not have one main building. Neither one corpus. Much rather it will be a corporation of different bodies housing a variety of corpora. A growing body of structures will be identified, which are or elude to potential to become part of the collection's estate. Bodies enclosing and contained will be literal and figurative. The collection's estate will be modular, operating on and off site. It will have multiple multiplying extensions. It will not be topologically anchored or static, but rather always growing, moving, appearing and disappearing.

The material structure of the collection will be constructed around the negative: holes, openings, rifts and clefts – leaving them gaping and visible as its main architectural feature. There will be neither glass panelling nor other forms of demarcations to barricade the apertures. Like wounds they will tear through the facade's skin, perforate walls and outer surfaces. The collection will be permeable to a maximum, no border walls be entirely closed, no demarcation completely intact, no walls continuous. Wind will blow and air circulate through the open holes deep into the hallways and rooms of the Collection of Un-healing. From the outside it will look like it contains nothingness, abandoned, vacant space. Its spaces will invite occupation and squatting. The collection will connect to sites of the negative – not in a qualitative sense – around which it will form. It will open everywhere. There will exist many ways in and out. Exits and entrances. No designated routes will be advised.

The appearance of the Collection of Un-healing's bodies will differ with each and every formation, changing from construction to construction. None will be alike, although they all share common characteristics. Assembled from natural, inexpensive, decomposing, broken, corrupt material, from the outside some will look like ruins, crumbling and sinking into the landscape's sediment. With others, the structures will appear incomplete, unfinished, in a process of becoming, while they will seem at the same time to exist or to enter into an inexorable state of decay.

Skeletal entablatures will support various structures precariously swaying, just balancing, resting on unsteady, oedematic foundations. Its surfaces wearing thin, carrying truncated fragments of other bodies, stutters and ruptures visibly rest on papery skin as put there hesitantly. Not all architectural bodies that comprise the collection will be physically tangible: hanging suspended in the air, quivering briefly, before fading and disappearing from sensory perception. Moving in sync with their surrounding, with what touches and passes them, some constructions might appear more fragile than they actually are. Some will say that the Collection of Un-healing appears sordid. Many will criticise its appearance on other grounds.

A partial gaunt physique, draped with leathery, waxy, soft skin, hanging and sinking, at parts drooping down by its own weight, at others stretched to the point of rupture, suspended between bones will be contrasted with bulging and swollen features. The collection's exterior surface will be discontinuous, interrupted by necrose, purulent, festering openings.

What may appear as a deterioration of structures is what in fact will contribute to the collection's metastatic growth and expansion all over the globe. The Collection of Un-healing stands in ignorance to borders and demarcations.

While the work of the Collection of Un-healing will be centred around lesions and holes, it is neither hospital, clinic nor even institution. Institutionalisation will not be in the interest of the collection, it doesn't busy itself with notions of cure. Care however is a different affair – both in the attempts of dressing and addressing of marks and inscriptions left on bodies the Collection of Un-healing will have gained a certain proficiency.

The internal atmosphere of the collection will be composed of vast dark, damp and gloomy spaces contrasted by narrow, winding tunnels, low, deep cavities, dim nooks, stretched hallways with walls running up on both sides. Interlinking doorways, holes and opening portals will intersect the continuous surface of the walling. Residual light falls inside through the perforated facades, through the incomplete, broken and corrupted structures of the shell of the Collection of Un-healing, painting shadow's edges blurry. The inside spaces will radiate warmth, breathe softly in rhythm with the visitors' movement through the interior. The spaces expand and contract in intervals of inhale and exhale, their moist walls will pulse gently.

Under its many roofs, inside its many rooms the collection will gather a multiplicity of concrete facilities ranging from archives, libraries, treatment centres, exhibits and displays, print rooms, spaces for collective assembly, places of worship and holey sites. Primarily though the Collection of Un-healing will be a space of and for voices: echoing, ricochetting until rising into a poly-vocal cacophony. Voices, low murmuring, minor and marginal will resound; discrepant, broken, truncated, word-shreds, sentence-rags and language-tatters, tethered to holes, circling both eloquently and articulate around negative space. They will fill the sites of the Collection of Un-healing, these voices. There will be no canon or harmony.

The collection will function as repository of words and voices, of experiences that do not easily manifest in language. Hence, simultaneously, although not paradoxically, the collection will also be a site of silence. Silent spaces that hold the inarticulate, the un-addressable, the unsayable together with other things that would be concealed, that fade out/disappear or are commonly not thought into existence to begin with.

The work of the Collection of Un-healing will be concerned with an accumulation of holey artefacts and relics. It will not only be conceived of a place of sole study or display but as a site of gathering and subversive resistance.

There will be no temporal order to the collection. Its sole focus will be on achronistic gatherings over and across temporalities. The Collection of Un- healing itself will try to remain mobile, transportable, through times and places. The collection will seek a polychronic, non-hierarchical, un-structured approach to its work and manifestation. It will operate in neglect of continuity, linearity, teleology and wholeness. There will be material flows in and out and through the collection continuously. It will not be able to fully contain its insides, nor does it aim for that. Its nature will be permeable, spilling, to remain in a constant exchange with its surrounding.

The Collection of Un-healing's attempt will be to gather and preserve what otherwise is lost. The broken, the ill, the destroyed, mere parts and fragments, pieces and nothingness, the lost and the lack. It will show that nothing is something. It might be criticised to follow an agenda of the un-whole. Some will always look for a non-existing totality. The Collection of Un-healing however doesn't ascribe itself to completeness.

The Collection of Un-healing will resist museification. No vitrines, plinths, and other museal forms of display will be encountered inside the collection. They will be rendered gratuitous for the specific artefacts of the collection. Concerning the inventory of the collection: commodification and property/ownership will be overturned. Nothing will belong to anyone specifically, all that enters the collection will be communal goods. Unsurprisingly the Collection of Un-healing will be unfunded. Its economical situation will be as precarious as its structures and contents. It will be a labour of love and pain, direct action and resistance to sustain this collection.

JALYNN HARRIS

I'LL KILL HIM MY OWN GAHTDAMN SELF!

*a lost image reclamation
after Anthony Cody*

1. osayim arrives in his pastry truck. a gun sleeps in the glove compartment
2. grandaddy spreads out like a wall between the bushes and the red door
3. mommy spikes the air with the love in her throat
4. in the top bunk, my brother holds a book like a knife
5. in the bottom bunk, my brother rubs his throbbing jaw
6. the glacial song of dial up
7. daddy sits at the desktop, clicking through chess matches
8. the bears on the wallpaper dance
9. i bang out notes on my organ. a clay figure at my ankle
10. love, the fire that calls her brother. love, the ice that guards the red door
11. a crab apple falls gently. scrambles the pine needles

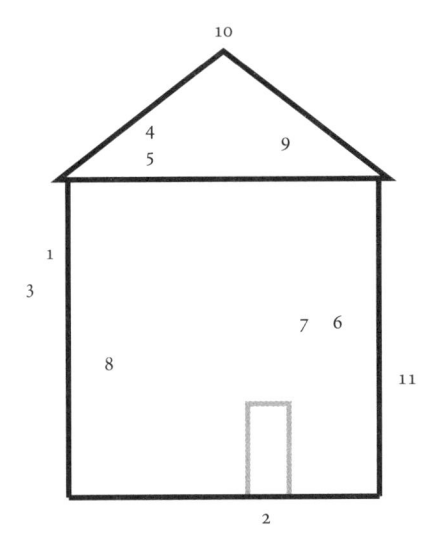

JACLYN DESFORGES

FLOWER GIRL

Your father is a series of photocopied fathers. He gets married, the way fathers do, and you aren't invited to the wedding. Your mother says *Daddy got married* and you'll remember her saying it in the house on Mary Street, but you'll look back and realize the timeline doesn't match, that you didn't live there for years after. Still, your memory takes place in the archway of the living room, near the radiator where the grey cat liked to sleep, near the couch where you first stayed home alone while your mother ran out to buy cough syrup. You'll remember the faxes he sent you on business trips, moustached self-portraits. You only climbed that backyard tree once. You only sat there for a minute. You see the wedding photo on his desk at one of his every-other-weekends. You were there, in a way, in some other dimension – you see yourself dropping rose petals, standing proudly in taffeta. *Can you tell her?* he must have asked your mother. She must have said *Yes*.

MAKSHYA TOLBERT

TREE WALK WITH WORRY

I worry even the violence is mycelial
and branches up   from the tree of each of us

I worry evenly   about the willow oaks   about what
spreads from all our petioles   I worry evenly

I try walking with the worry   Some's mine   some's not
Heat lamps eat away at the willow oaks

Meanwhile   I don't eat   beholden to the accidental
violence of what we don't notice   I barely notice

I worry   I willow   sweltering through the changes
I worry
   I willow   I shake my throat

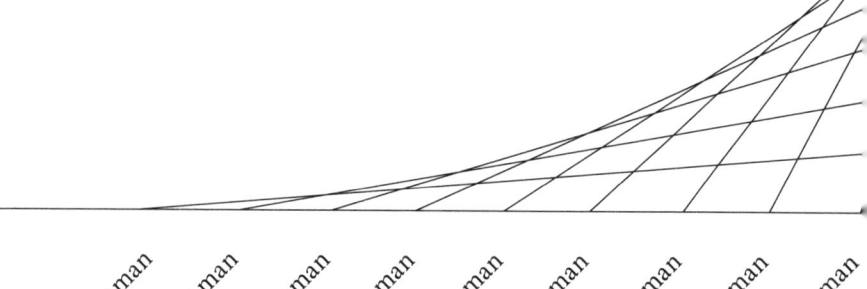

LILLIAN-YVONNE BERTRAM

DOOMSDAY GRID

D

O

O

M

S

D

A

Y

a white man   a white man   a white man   a white man   a white man   a white man   a white man   a white man   a white man   a white man walks into my office unzips his fly wants resume help

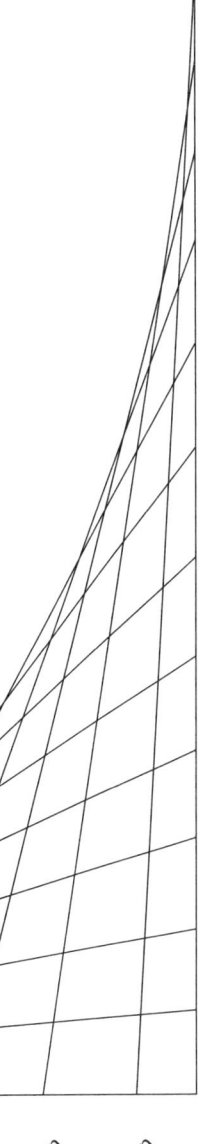

with mommy issues walks into my office demands an
active spectator sniffs around wants sex sniff sniff sniff

walks into my office needs some parenting

with his business face on walks into my office asks
to move in make a baby and a happy ending

with his dick out walks into my office says hey doctor
black lives matter black lives matter black lives matter

walks into my office asks me to front him till payday
says sorry steals my car begs again

with his name on the screen walks into my office needs
help teaching his class asks why u so mad

with money problems walks into my office needs needs
needs

walks into my office asks me to explain the assignment

walks into my office with his white wife says
wanna be poly with me huh huh huh

walks into my office with his daddy issues

walks into my office won't leave won't grow creates
nothing

CHAUN WEBSTER

from WITHOUT TERMINUS

saying some names feels as though you are drawing a character, a sketch. always incomplete. the messy lines being drawn inevitably crack, pasts leaking from their fissures. what are the rules of kinship here? what are the rules of imagining kin, of calling your gone as though they are more than once bodies, than bare life? what does it mean when the train and miles of track, when steam and coal and freight car are all notations on the character, written over them like a second skin? what happens when the train and some more-than-bodied kin are indistinguishable?

you spend a lot of time thinking about loss, considering if what is missing has a form, wondering if there is a method to tracing what is not visible. there was a time when you thought that if you just had greater powers of imagination, or if you could somehow place yourself securely along the tracks of family and cultural history that you could gather sufficient evidence, collect all the bones to make something of a complete structure. now i only debate on whether to move through the impossibility of recuperation with my own limited attempt to exhume through vernacular, an act necessitating its own failure, or to search for what seems equally impossible: a means to write my own dead with a grammar that recognizes that loss is without teleology.

you had a maternal grandfather. Reginald Jerry Clark. dead eight years and a day prior to your birth. read backwards you were a grandchild, to a Clark, who is gone, was dead. he is a porter for The Great Northern Railroad.

you've known him in a photo, arched forward on a couch with his eyes closed. it seems important to say he is working in the sleeping car, that he will labor for 25 years. there is a past where your mother, Reginald's daughter, tells you he hates this job, was hated, is equal parts invisible and not, will swallow whole train cars of bitterness, will have become a ghost. it seems important to say he is working 25 years and has retired without pension, is working in the sleeping car, will have had no rest over three hours that is not deducted from pay.

you have a child who is fascinated with trains—read backwards—there is a great grandchild to your maternal grandfather, who was employed by the train, with this fascination.

after the track is laid and the train cars are placed on them your child will repetitively position something ahead of the car's arrival, several blocks or a book or a body part. they love watching the collision. sometimes you hear them in the other room, laughing at another derailing.

up until the 1920's it was common practice to derail a train in order to prevent a collision, but as trains grew heavier and faster, they could continue to accumulate damage, could continue to collide.

in *Glissant and the Middle Passage* John E. Drabinski writes that, *piles of wreckage are still history,* and this might be the case, you might be able to collect every piece of rubble and rumor, every shadow and slanted rendering of your grandfather's name or maybe the desire to make something whole of what is collected is misguided. maybe history is a poor tool for collecting ghosts, besides, you are more invested in holes than history.

there is something about the speed and weight of your subject, the accumulated damage to his body that lacks a proper name. collision is a moving object violently striking against another, but what has struck him is not condensed steel, it is a world which has its condition of possibility in his unmaking, in him being the hollow place where others construct the terms of ontology. there is something about the holes, the supposed not-thereness of your kin that is as dense as the past.

perhaps the entry then is theft. perhaps theft is where you should begin. which is to say absence is the point of departure. you enter from what is absented.

this is to move forwards, and backwards too. something is always being stolen. consumed. a repast, a table of sumptuous remains.

and it is ruins, the imagined potential for some thing to be ruined that shapes the grammar of value for insurance.

you are always coming back here, to the departure you are always arriving at.

here, being a language of proximity. arrival, a language of debris.

you are always imagining ruin.

your grandfather worked the rail, the labor and what was done to bear it undid him at a cellular level. your grandfather was the rail, was a porter, laboring 25 years, was the steam engine working whistling, howling, was the rail, was retired without pension, the wallet he left you is empty he was the rail, was the service hands working was the wreckage, was undone is gone. this is not called theft. yet you are certain something has been stolen. you are the evidence.

you wonder if you are the rail also.
if you are also the wreckage.

you are a living ruins, an archive of lost things.

SPAM EATER

composed of fragments from the poet's spam folder

create and   manage   attack groups   the family
make the next one even better   Asians   hold Catholic values
   phonetic spelling   in the name of the father and of the son
                            and of the   hoary   spirit
   every devotion   wow-worthy
     on both sides
the new platform   act fast   not responsible for typographical errors
awe   men
          limited time   unspoken   anger
apology for the racial   cardboard
traditional   stewards of   perinatal   transaction
seven-thousand-plus islands   three-thousand-plus   shoes
  we love   the Philippines   service experience
  we love   God's timing   beard   the recent election
our community   ends today
the story behind   activate here   explore here   reset here   please join
kneel   please   problems
       explore   the South China Sea
it's arriving soon   it's almost gone   our hearts
   deviant   factory   sanctity   the reality is
yellow
                        we are here if you need help

NATURALLY NO

plastic	nothing	ching	
snore	prepared	piano	
no	time	elbow	
bone	obstacle	oracle	
Suddenly	list	en	
sud	denly	sneeze	
brush	&	brush	
turns	&	brush	
sugar	&	brush	
salt	method	,	
glass	whack	desiree	
sonata	shaggy	nag	Naturally No
rubber	hiss	possess	
also	eye	ching	
technique	technik	tec-nik	
que		?	
one:	any	ears	
sneeze un		fortunately	
metal	climax	p	
timpani	nothing	m	
deaf	bush	z	
crops	up	q	
fungusfugues		wood	
piano	sound	paper	
no	sound	no	
so	O	so	

MAX GREGG

HOMOSEXUALITY ("CURES")

Everyone dreams every night—even if they don't remember it.
      —*Man's Body: An Owner's Manual* (1976)

                If the sleeper is woken
                a many-celled abnormality

              sometimes severely

            shaken into
                    the shape of
                            the market

            prophesy the future and

            comment on the hormones

            a) male hormone, far from
            making   homo   more
            "masculine"   makes vivid the
            desire for whatever average Dreams.
                                in
                                    vertiginous

            movement a purple pigment
                  impotence and   such

            In any case: attachments)
                ethical conjunctiva   now
            interfering with the hormone
            it overflows and it falls down the face

It may be that reasons for taking drugs
outnumber   Breakfast cereals.   If woken in this way if woken

   it has not been   so as to amplify the
proven   present and past

normal deviancy   struggle to find pleasure in collisions
rests on the assumption
      that homo is a
great heat, which spreads deep
      that it can
be easily changed

     a disturbance a Blockage
a protective action may be introduced
female seduction   with a fallen lash, the aesthetic is
"anxiety-free" with   a warm wax
      usual   hardening

"aversion therapy", a patient   Light bleaches
    shown pictures of nude men   (the process is fluid
and given an electric shock   that stymies patient
injection inducing unintelligible   noise
also he will have no memory   memory

        memory   finally proved a pounding
a displaced outlet   now a crude and halting   a chronic
plan   escaping sex as   stretched   endurance
material   if   unintelligible

BRENDA SHAUGHNESSY

TELL OUR MOTHERS WE TELL OURSELVES THE STORY WE BELIEVE IS OURS

1.

The women created
the tunnels and the caves
for everyone.

Offering home or a place to hide,
space to be. To be held or hid
or helped to become old.

Blue stone, in nature,
is a trick of the eye,
a sky-trick, light playing air,

sky-diving into earth
to make you see it,
even if it's not there.

2.

"Now Dad's gone you can have fun."

"I could learn to have fun,
but I might never succeed,
and it seems like a waste of whatever
else I could have a chance to learn."

"Like puzzles? A new language?"

"Fun doesn't have to be learned
at all if you have it young enough.
But me—I'd have to work at it.
I don't know how to have fun."

She said that
as if someone else had said it to her.

3.

So I said: "Who told you
you 'don't know how to have fun?'"

"What?"

"You said 'One problem with me
is I don't know how to have fun,'

Did someone tell you that about yourself
or is that your own self-knowledge?"

"I think someone told me: you don't know
how to have fun

and I'd never thought about it before: fun.
My life was never fun.

I was a child and children have fun but
not me. Nobody looked after me
and I didn't even have the basics—
not enough was all I knew.

So when someone (your dad) told me
I didn't know 'how to have fun' of course

I believed him.

It was true. That's how I came to believe it,
I think, because of the truth of it. And also because
your dad said it was true."

But it can't be both.
But it can't be separated.

4.

CHAIN MAIL

If you do not copy this letter and mail it to six of your closest heart-friends (who adore you and think you'd have better judgment than to do this) you will experience radical misfortune that looks like fun/luck, (not the sad event that nevertheless yields a golden river dawn.) The following is just an example:

When the ceiling drops
the rain stops
beating down but
now you're beaten down

though it's the beat
that drops now
and we dance
in the rain
like sunbeams
made out of metal cloth,
tubes of blood,
and scared, sewn-up eyes.

5.

Then Dad left—
well . . . did he actually leave?

When he was with us he was intensely absent,
But when he physically left it seemed
he was effortlessly still there, still   "with us?"

There must be a difference,
and it can't be both
since one is fact (he left)
and one is fiction. (he's here)

One is an act
and one is addiction.

6.

A story of how we travel   (because we want to or need to,
                                   rarely both.)

from painful lost-in-the unknown   (are you my mother?)

and being left out   (in the rain, of the circle, to rot.)

to finding love   (which includes endlessly morethan
                                   what's contained by the word of it but
                                   that container holds the map to find it.)

to finding love within   (the longest journey has the same repeatin
                                   terrain—switchbacks, backtracks, circles—
                                   only to end up mere paces from the start.)

to making the world without   (is a magic. to imagine and to wonder
reflect the world within   fiercely, is this what we're meant to do
                                  in this life?)

and vice versa   (or is there something else?
                                  or is this only for artists?)

to heal both   (is this what we're meant to do
entry and exit wounds   in this life?)
to repair the path between

but what if the path remains
broken, the wounds open

and the world wasn't reflected
either to or from itself

neither made nor made of

and we didn't find love within
and we didn't find love
and we weren't left out
so we didn't feel lost and alone
so we never traveled
but stayed here,
whether we wanted to
or needed to   (does that difference make all the difference?)

to try to find our true story.   (which may be nowhere, it's true.)

7.

Oh but what is the story, after all that?
it's not a straight line or a jagged one.

It's a spray cloud,
        fast water hitting rock hard
        and exploding,
        then coming together to
        settle back and go
        the original direction
        toward the sea.

The story is many spray clouds
            and storm clouds
                  wind storms, the breath of trees
                  and other living things, off-gassing.
Clouds of natural gas.
Hot air. Cool breeze. Naturally. Unnaturally.

                But nothing's natural.
                And nothing's unnatural either.
                The original concept is off.
                Switched off.

Switch it on: that story is winding
both ways,
a short story that's taking forever.

8.

The story is a family
of inside and outside,

who begat grass underfoot
and green recycled siding,

who adopted wind energy
and gas guzzling. And invasive
species married in—

and winter vegetables
divorced out.

The heat and the cold grew up
unsupervised, basically, and can't
feel anything.

The flowers so automatically
attached themselves to your leg
as you try to run away

to find another shelter
you can afford
where, if time turns out
to be a good roommate,
you won't have to immediately
make plans to move again,

a thing that's called "to stay."

If we keep saying it,
the story might stay   (if it doesn't turn away from us)
and make its home in us,
will travel with us,   (unravel us)
will begin to understand
the family of itself
as it is delivered to us   (living in a grotto, moving to a cave,
as we are delivered to it.   through a tunnel a woman made.)

9.

Women cupped their hands
to make baskets

to catch babies
to carry and carry.

Women made the vessels
the tub the cup the jug
the mug, many things
with U in it, held by her
making and making.

Women made the jars
and pitchers to pour
themselves into,
to pour for you,
pouring and pouring
for everyone.

10.

The story is a rage/range
of hills and mountains,
—anger dispersed over years
years ago—

that look and feel like a reclining
woman and nobody is offended
by this anymore.

Resting in middle age for energy
to make everything for everybody,
shortly, longingly.

She's the main character even though
she doesn't travel.

She is the traveled.

SAFIA ELHILLO

THE ROOM

What bothers me today is that I cannot remember. In the Zamalek apartment, in Cairo, I remember all the rooms but one. Front entrance, kitchen immediately to the left, on whose door I once cut my ankle and trailed long meters of blood into the other rooms. Dining table just outside the kitchen's second entrance, where I sat for Arabic lessons, revolted to distraction by the tutor's adam's apple, sliding over his throat like the bead of an abacus when he took tea. Beyond it, living room, sofas arranged inward, long couch on which I slept the eve of Eid and waited for whoever brought the presents, knowing we had no Santa Claus but believing my cousin when she told me for Muslims it was Xena, Warrior Princess. A scarf over her breasts. The door to Shihab's room in the back right corner, always closed, cavern of cigarette smoke and computer games, the first time I heard hip hop, a man in a dark suit and sunglasses speaking to a dead friend, a woman with dark brown lipstick missing you. Back toward the front door, the staircase leading down. Bottom floor where my brother and I played under the stairs until sunset, the gloaming hour when my grandmother said the veil was thinnest, the jinn listening. To the right the bathroom where we were bathed in a shared tub and sang invented songs. To the left a smaller living room for the young adults. Just ahead of it Issraa's room where she bleached her hair and studied theater, wore Kookaï and practiced lines for The Tempest. To the right my grandparent's room, enormous to me then, my grandmother at her dressing table trying to comfort me, my heartbreak over yet another infected ear piercing closing up. Trying to explain how I felt. That without earrings I could never be a girl. Where my brother and I unearthed a pedicure kit while playing and I removed one of his toenails with a metal tool. Every room accounted for except the one. I lived there, years of uniforms at the British school, my grandmother buying me Jelly Cola on the walk home, violin and Arabic and straightening my hair for picture day. We lived there, my mother my brother and I, in a room in that apartment, and my memory has taken it from me. I walk through it again, front door kitchen living room, Shihab, staircase, bathroom, living room, Issraa, my grandparents. And still my memory stops. I cannot remember, for all those years, all the nights of all those years, the room in which I slept.

MAHOGANY L. BROWNE

THE 19TH AMENDMENT & MY MAMA

I always took it for granted, the right to vote
She said
And I knew what my mother meant
Her voice constricted tightly by the flu A virus
& a 30-year-relationship
with Newport 100s
I ain't no chain smoker
she attempts to silence my concern
only a pack a week. That's good, you know?
My mother survived a husband she didn't want

and an addiction that loved her more
than any human needs

I sit to write a poem about the 100 year Anniversary
of the 19th Amendment
& my first thought returns to the womb
& those abortions I did not want at first
but alas

The thirst of an almost anything
is a gorge always looking to be
until the body is filled with more fibroids
than possibilities
On the 19th hour of the fourth day in a new decade
I will wake restless from some nightmare
about a bomb & a man with no backbone

on a golf course who clicks closed his Motorola phone
like an exclamation point against his misogynistic stance
He swings the golf club with each chant
Women let me grab
Women like me
Women vote until I say they don't

In my nightmare he is an infective agent
In the clear of day
he is just the same

Every day he breathes is a threat to this country's marrow
For Ida & Susan & Lucretia & Elizabeth Cady

& every day he tweets grief
like a cynical cornball comic's receipts
like a red light signaling the end of times

The final night of 2019
& my New Year's Eve plans involves
anything that will numb the pain
of a world breaking its own heart

My mother & I have already spoken
& her lungs are croaking wet
I just want you to know I don't feel well
& I pause to pull up my stockings beneath my crumpled smile
On this day I sigh
I just wanted to dance & drink & forget about the 61.7% votes

My silk dress falls to my knees with the same swiftness
defiant as the white feminist who said "I'm your ally"
then voted for the demise of our nation's most ignored
underpaid, imprisoned & impoverished citizens

Every day there is a telephone near
I miss my mother
In the waiting room of the OB/GYN
Uptown bound on the dirt orange train seat of the subway
O! How my mother loves the places she can never go
Her bones swaddled with arthritis & smoke
So she relies on my daily bemoans

The train smells like yesterday, Ma
They raise the tolls & fix nothing for the people
My landlord refuses to fix my toilet, my bathroom sink, my refrigerator
The city is annoying like an old boyfriend, always buzzing about nothing
& in the way of me making it on time to the polls
This woman didn't say thank you when I held the door
& who does she think she is?

Each time I crack & cap on the everydayness of my day
My mother laughs as if she can see the flimsy MTA card
The yellow cabs that refuse to stop for her daughter
In these moments she can live again
A whole bodied woman with a full mouth
to speak it plain
I ask my mother what hurts?
What hurts?
How can I help from here?

3000 miles away
Alone in a tower between the sea
& the Mexico borders

My mother sighs a little sigh & says
Nothing
I just wanted to hear your voice

STEFANIA GOMEZ

THE KEEPER

for Gert McMullin, AIDS Quilt Conservator

A disco ball
                        full of ashes

— — —

A sewing machine   name of Connie

    strewn among fifty others   like old Chevys

        a graveyard

— — —

A hundred thousand panels   60 tons   each the size and shape of a grave

— — —

These are my boys
        that's what I call them
                my boys

— — —

To make a quilt (machine)   one cut the main fabric   two cut contrast fabric
three sew contrast fabric   four iron fabric   five pin and sew main fabric
six trim the batting   seven sew the quilt backing   eight cut the backing
assemble the quilt   nine stitch   ten bind

— — —

Me   I severed myself   from my name   re-christened   1985 a kind of mercy
for who I was   before   my story unstitched   in the wards at SF General
across ten blocks in the Castro   a thousand   seams   ripped

— — —

Born   1985   November 27   seven years after Harvey Milk's murder
the thousandth death   a candlelight march   to the Federal Building   on
its face   we arranged   a thousand placards

    a patchwork   of names

— — —

"She just pretty much turned over her whole life to that project   She would
work all day, and then climb up into one of the shelves and fall asleep with the
quilt, and then get up and start over again."

— — —

To make a quilt (by hand)   one collect materials   two
prewash fabric   three iron   four measure and cut   five
sew patchwork   six measure   seven iron   eight sew
nine stitch   ten bind

— — —

The only rule the name the initials beyond that I take any decoration for the dead

— — —

        A lightbulb   pony sticks   hypodermic needle

— — —

Over a hundred panels   of men I knew   some whose deaths I stumbled upon   on a panel   so many more   unknowns   lives I discovered   only to grieve them

— — —

    Best fabrics for quilting   home décor weight cotton
    quilter's weight cotton   essex linen voile quilter's
    linen

— — —

When you live through something   they call you lucky

— — —

    A dozen piano keys   an AC filter   "God broke our hearts"
    a varsity jacket, whole   floral fabric in Nevada's shape
    "June 10 1985 –   June 30 1993"

— — —

I am lucky   for the friends that live   in the panels   the panels the same as my life   where each day I'm sewn   and sewn with debt

— — —

    Types of quilt designs   Anchorage   Arkansas
    traveler   bear paw   cabin fever   Celtic cross
    Celtic square charm   crumb   disappearing

        drunkard's path   fat quarter   flying geese
        fresh diamonds   granny's square   jungle path
        lattice   square   log cabin   nine patch   patch-
        work   rainbow   log cabin   seven pointed star
        sixteen patch   Smokey   Mountain   star   star
        flower   wedding ring

— — —

What obsesses me   is the damage   the shredding panels   all across the floor   slice   re-hem   re-grommet   a day's work   until at last   I fall asleep with it   within it

— — —

In the warehouse where it lives I feel safe like nothing nothing could happen

— — —

Skin in purple archipelagos fungus reaches the brain hearing at last leaves a shrinking pile of foil-wrapped candy in a corner of a room

— — —

My hands on each panel I walked through each door in the ward listened to each story

— — —

        To remember   one collect materials   two cut and
        assemble   three trim the backing   become   batting
        four measure   loss   five sew what remains   six log
        cabin   charm   crumb   disappearing   seven   linen
        voile   quilter's weight   eight sew   nine stitch   ten
        bind

— — —

One hundred thousand panels   60 tons   unbelievable the   weight   of absence

— — —

A bouquet of ties   years embroidered in chenille

      angel wings   flaming magenta

            condom wrappers   patterned like stars

KATHY WU

WERNER'S NOMENCLATURE OF

Something darwinian—
    a [Object]
    a
perhaps a planar
 color which suffers and
animal, vegetable, mineral distinctly
foment the blue-er sea, take
up tenancy in letters, we
reject the colonial found, swear
on absence of light: is white's color
Junction of, Breast of [Object]

Spectrum blanks in hand—
    Neck and Back of the Kittiwake Gull
    White Geranium, Storks Bill Arragonite
    Egret Hawthorn Blossom Chalk & Tripoli
    White or Screech Owl, Large Wild Convolvulus
    French Porcelain Clay Skimmed Milk
    Human Eyeballs Back of the Petals Blue
    Hepatica Common Opal
    a

Can it be—
    Throat of
    Stamina
    Beauty Spot

LORRAINE RICE

OF BEING WILL & TESTAMENT

(from the last will and testament of William J. Reynolds, in which he bequeaths the bulk of his estate to Lavinia Brisbane (formerly enslaved) and her/their children — Sumter, SC, 1884)

ITEM 1st: Mind the knot of memory the body keeps; mind the land, being more or less the last testament to the memory of a name, a body, the will to give housekeeper (more or less wife), and the heirs of her body, acres to last and keep the mind sound.

ITEM 2nd: Will the keeper of the house her house, her land, her acres to mind and keep for the body being more her body.

ITEM 3rd: Name the swampmind of Men, and her (HouseKeeperWife) being of more sound mind and memory.

ITEM 4th: Name her being.

ITEM 5th: Watch the daughter mill a memory to give her body a name, a sound less wife, more will.

ITEM 6th: Give the daughter acres of memory and watch her knot the swamp, body the house, and mind the heirs – testament to her being.

ITEM 7th: Knot the name to the body and the body to the land.

ITEM 8th: Give testament to the last house of being, sound the memory and swamp the acres: her name   *wife*   the heirs of her body   *Amen.*

ITEM 9th: Give, mind, watch, will and Men will mill the knot to memory,

ITEM 10th: or less.

FAMILY HISTORY IN ABSTRACT
(after a collection of headlines from various US newspapers, 1887)

    I.   from *The Emporia Daily Globe*, 15 July 1887, p. 1

> **One of the Wealthiest South Carolina Farmers Dies and Leaves His Wealth to His ~~Colored Concubine~~ and Mulatto Children — The Amount $600,000.**

> This is a story of ownership — false starts and bad seeds that sour the soil and never yield, bear fruit, or even flower, assuming they survive at all. Histories are rife with bottomless hunger: who starves, who feeds. This story begins the same, with theft, brutality, and accumulation — Is it better or worse to be so familiar with how this goes, the weft and weave? Only, by the end it seems there was some epiphany following a near-drowning in the swamp. She dove in and rescued him. I like to think she just reached out a hand; the other held fast to a knotted branch.

II. from *The Scranton Republic*, 20 Jul 1887, p. 2

A Relic of Slavery Days
*

What remains? What salvaged shards and reparations — interrupted, the way the light obstructs at sunset, deceives, makes everything gold — even the bones of this family arc. What compensation? What remnants break the earth and bloom like bruises against anemic sky — and under the skin, blood blistering. What anthropologist am I? Sifting these blue-tinged brittle bits, reading the scars of fracture — parsing the meaning of repair.

III. from *The New York Times*, 14 Jul 1887, p. 1

FIGHTING FOR A FORTUNE: THE STRANGE STORY OF THE LIFE OF

A woman with no land in her chart, no inheritance to claim, apart from ghosts and the deep imprint of loss — genetic memory of the cheat older than the moss under my father's feet — desiccated shells pinned to a thin white sheet at the last. Once upon a life there was another life and so on down the line, or up the spiral spring, holy green circling back to winter-faded fields. Knife-edged wind to test the will of stone fathers, ineluctable crumble, and hearty daughters who carry the ashes in the creases of their palms and legacy. The story stirs still, unfolding as I breathe.

IV. from *The Newberry Herald and News*, 28 Jul 1887, p. 4

THE END OF A BLIGHTED CAREER — DEATH
~

One blighted end is another beginning — birth and death inextricable. One life bleeding into the next, muddied streams flowing forward and back to the source, before this course of events. A man dies aged, embracing four thousand acres, several children, a wife, the papers claim. Three turns and a son dims, inefficiently broke, in an efficiency overlooking ghost structures, sentinels on the land where joy and grief used to dance and wail. What eminent domain claimed you, Father, in a high rise doomed for demolition? Flesh and stone bodies worn by attrition.

V. from *The Emporia Daily Globe*, 15 July 1887, p. 1

Anger of the Relatives and Threats to Invalidate The Will — the Biography
*

On the bridge from now to then, this technicolor hour arced to sepia-tinged days lasting years, folded into milkweed moments, goldenrod and fire pink, I am fanning the flames higher, hotter, brighter so when the softwood, rot-riddled, is cleared I can build again, plank by sturdy plank until I reach the land promised — More myth than memory — but she is my true destination. She who remains unwritten in their pages, misnamed: *colored concubine illegitimate wife slave.* Her name is Lavinia, and it is her story, her will I tease from this tangle of roots.

THE MAP AS MISDIRECTION

Who deeds the vellum atlas of origin? We're in here praise-dancing against its borders: ream, river, mountain range. There is no imperial nation-state without imp–the devil ripping accords, eyes refusing contact. Freedom :: full moon : REDACTED (and wouldn't you like to know, they waggle). We remind you that poems are not aid packages and the boys can be road plans too—slick-wet oil thumbs. The red push pins now polaroids faded to white plastic. The ghost of a town with the trash still buzzing.

LILLIE WALSH

ACCORDED A NEW RECOLLECTION

Archival accessioning is a formal process of ownership transfer, from a source to a collection. Accession numbering is a method of organization that notates both ownership and provenance of any given artifact within a collection. Accession numbers are also used to locate an individual artifact within a larger collection.

This piece has been created in the traditional form of archival accessions. This is being used as both an organizational structure as well as a method of complicating the legality, ownership, and hierarchy of order that the mode invokes.

As they speak to each other each accession will continue to reshuffle their contents. Some will appear empty, only upon first glance.

This is where memory will be held, performed, and instructed. In order to map the ways in which memory is housed and tucked away for later use a cast of objects will appear here.

ACCESSION 2388.01 - PLACE
This becomes the realm of the spatial, what container is given to the players at hand for comprehensive transmission. The container becomes its own modality of telling. The parsing between the boxes and the piles is here.

ACCESSION 2388.02 - OBJECT RELATIONS IN PRACTICE
What are your wooden spoons talking about when you're not in the room? Objects will perform themselves for you to the point of environmental totality. Touch becomes a practice of deep listening here, sensory input cross firing

into a net of communication between organic and inorganic body. You are not immune to the way in which a bouquet of flowers is an interaction with itself, the performance is inescapable.

ACCESSION 2388.03 - AND TELL ME AGAIN ABOUT THING POWER
This is an eavesdrop, really. Orchestrated dinner table conversation by means of choosing the place setting and the pot that holds the clams with the utmost conviction of (their ability to) interchange.

ACCESSION 2388.04 - CHARTING THE CATALOG
The framework to be found here arrives by way of citational practice. To cup the ephemerality, to sit in a circle with the rest of them.

ACCESSION 2388.05 - NO TITLE (ONE OF ONE)
More detail, please. In an effort to relearn how to utilize all of my surfaces, time spent here will stretch between an open palm and a shoulder turned.

When taken out of the institutions from which they are usually relegated and placed in the context of artistic inquiry, archival objects utilized are offered two new opportunities: a different environment from which to communicate -this implies something like more space to breathe- and the understood legitimacy as capturers of memory and cultural moment by being placed in a container deemed archival.
Recognizing the ability of objects to exert a certain force and affect on proximate bodies fixes their role in the archive beyond just that as a tool of historical narration. It extends the container into a living scene of players, those that can be in active dialogue with persons reading the collection. This suggests that perhaps beyond the realms of our human knowing these objects, enacting their thing-power, are having dialogue between themselves. And in the context of the scene of the archive, extend this conversation to represent what we the readers interpret as historical record.

14k gold, pearls, garnet. ½ inch by 1 inch. Approximately between 1820 and 1914. A memorial ring, set in gold and framed with seed pearls, centering a garnet engraved with a lily of the valley flower.

A gift of announcement, I was on the way then. Or maybe I had just arrived. This is an era of knowing beyond asking, a shared intimacy of one another's specificities. Recently bent, I stopped wearing it to work. There is an impulse to wear the exquisite into the ground, to take it with me. Reaching along the axis of two bays it only pulls back and back again. There is a twinning within its oneness, a split. Given and given again. The first time the act of noticing, the second a nonaction of maternal imprint.

Q. Does it fit under your tongue?

Paper, silver and light pink, ribbon. Handmade crown, material thicker than cardstock, thinner than cardboard. Bent and stained. 2005.

Objects that are brought out once a year hold memory differently. In such close tandem with only allotted time, their performance becomes regimented. What they hold is often more reliable. How quick do I have to be to shift it, how long can I make the morning to do so?

Q. What is the sound of disintegrating paper?

Wood. Soft and light in color. 2001 (*Date made up and imagined*). Carved olive spoon. Cracked along the slotted bowl and chipped in two places.

It was often a site of entertaining at high production value. The detail of tablecloth fretted over, the potatoes and spoons tossed with the comfort of someone who has been doing this for years. Table set for fourteen. Out on the grass. Lilac waft. Tide in or out.

It was often just us in the house. She painted our living room plum color and the front door bright orange. 'Peace is healthy for children and other living things' stuck on the glass of it.

This is where I learned to catalog objects by weight a▮▮▮▮▮▮▮

There are two panoramic photos crookedly taped together in the center. You can see the windowsill and the bluff and the mountains and the bay. The edges of the island. 'View from Lillie's Bedroom, November 1998.' I got there the next month.

Now I remember that wooden olive spoons are very light.

Q. What does it feel like when you squeeze as tight as you can?

Hand painted and lacquered Noritake porcelain. 3 inches x 2 inches. Approximately 1940s. A container in the shape of a swan. No lid.

It sits at my window and watches as I type, as I eat my breakfast. It arrived with a visitor. No, it was mailed to my apartment just after the visitor. No, it was handed to me. One from a snapped shut era that taught me to note the stamp on the bottom. A new method of timekeeping. It could hold matches, hairpins, it asks for stick shaped companionship. The ecology of porcelain this thing is born from was a catalyst of shared language. Beyond language, actually. It set off a seriesof swapped images until we realized we were not speaking to each other anymore.

Q. What is the shape of the object's shadow?

ESTHER G. BELIN

REVOLT OF THE RE-TERRITORIALIZED TONGUE

I.

I have been reading the reports, the long-handed riveted ripples penned from officers of the U.S. military (institution of colonial domain) tamping down Indigenous blood-shed, tissue, bone and ornament as meal, as fertilizer to Creator-given soil

       I have been reading the reports with my peripheral brain – my cognitive creative brain is too Precious, too much on this side of recovery, this side of sunsets protected from the asphalt seamed-in asphyxiated stories

       I have been reading the reports wearing my helmet of Salvation pulled tightly around my crown –– calling upon the Monster Slayers to slash the syllables from my tongue, to gut the colonial syntax – bring the savage poetics of Diné bizaad back to the shoreline of my vocabulary, oxygenating my lifeblood

Reports I have been re-arranging like outdated dioramas, plastering over exposed flesh, moistening the dehydrated voices, pruning the colonized contorted roots – unsettling the placid punctuated Phrases with surgical pincers, reordering the syllabics, hand-stitching the mangled lining of my tongue

       I have been grammaring myself into this syntactical remembrance, digging up myself from the colonized Redaction

II.

More commonly known as the U.S. Colorado-New Mexico state border.

The 37°N parallel becomes the boundary line dividing the two union states and is approximately 334 miles long.

Colorado was admitted to the Union on August 1, 1876, becoming the 38th state. New Mexico was admitted to the Union on January 6, 1912, becoming the 47th state. The Union has yet to admit bloodguiltiness.

The division created from state lines and the settler occupation of this region does not extinguish Indigenous territory. The fraudulent principles of the Doctrine of Discovery sifts the Chaff from the genocidal threshing, grates humanity into the ink in racial-inspired computations, Congressional, Military-insertions, slight negations, fractionated Semantics – crossing blood, crossing land – stolen, pioneered, pierced, prodded, punctuated, pummeled – excavated, extracted, then eliminated with boundary lines.

III.

                      The contents map loss: _____ & _____
           _____ & _____ , _____ & _____
    machine-gunned
groanings
tumble out
letters

    adjust the volume on the decibel   while
filling in the blanks   (more & more)   less multiples of choice
the letter K funnels last year's fits of rage into
the lower case I pries layers of skin, injects addictive substances
the L dams things up – wedges into sharp-corners, hooks & loops limbs
the second letter L – repeats the action with more velocity

The empty (blank) spaces are not a loss – The empty is reloading the long-barrel
    hunting rifle
and I let it fill me up
and shape me

IV.

May this Legislative War its prescriptive 2x/day
syringe-administered granular syntax
         (and its offspring too) seize

    coal-rouged cheeks
    uranium-sooted eyelids
    viral-pink painted lips

Kidnapper of Women

Overgrazing on our syllabic iotas perfunctory poison
         its doing

A poison is a poison is a poison is truth leaving everything behind

    A poison is a poison is a poison is a substance with many aliases, contorting tongue & territory, a false-faced historically-used schematics scratching away [the surface]
[Indigenous] origins

         (legislatively prescribed)

A poison is a command to play my harp for the King

    May   war &[its]offspring   Seize

SASHA BURSHTEYN

LAMINATION

The Natural Wonders are a set of political motivations inscribed onto landscape. Steppe // city // lake // lake // biosphere // desert // canyon // become metaphors for the nation. Nation = waterfall. Nation = granite. Logic pursues its own forked tail over dirt roads and onto pavement; its wheels are   all-terrain.   All border towns are contraband, all English comes from the rightmost side, all headstones are bright blue. Therefore it follows that fish = locals / coins =lamentation / electricity = rain / living = green / machine = stone / spirit = sewage.   Do you follow?   Do you read me?   Right there, where your foot is, you can dig   the city, of course, beautiful, by rain   a decision that was more war   a dynamo economist   a little bit non-linear   she's going to tell us more about   he would like to interject again   we are a crucial part of the drinking supply   for all of your cranes!   You move on / to the / great knowledge / super hard to produce.   I have to say that summer was not / sleep was not / borders were not / pine was not / motion was not / clay was not / pleasure was not / wonder was not. What I see live on the edge is that we are a kitchen for all of Europe. that is / territory.   Where on the water? is hard to answer.   If it's raining, drink, fry fish, hang out, play cards.   If archeological evidence is not enough, invent some.   If you'd like to visit a 100,000 year old drunk   brought here by a glacier, the map can take you there. I'm being shown ancient coins and cranes' nests at the tops of telephone poles.

PANORAMA OF LIGHT

Tremendous myth
          engulfed Donbas.

The steppe kissed the crowd.

      Incarnations worked the soil.

Anthracite crawled
          and strained,
     an evil gossip of dirt.

The coal had power—savage
capital.

Shrewd summer— red contradiction—

Hence the whip remained.

*

A contemporary image suggested fatigue.

Ringing bells reported
        unbridled exploitation.

Imagery was mythology,
        tilled land a logic,
the soil a rare extravagance.

The steppe kissed the crowd.

An exodus attracted fish
          and rituals of local momentum.

Coal mining announced
the climate: murderous, dull.

Weary undulations
torn by hot wind.

*

Ethics were essential,
       a modern incarnation
of imagined wildness.

Seasonal labor
             consumed
             the workers.

Coal mining
           announced
           the climate.

Miners substituted living
for astonishing metallurgy,
        kissing the language.

*

Imagery tilled the land.

Secondhand living
was the reputation.

The most famous was the official.
    Hence, discrete fact.

  Hence, the rational self.

Chronic water,
sulfur and smoke.

Industrial theater of the plant.

I expressed my Luhans'k.
    I kissed the crowd.

In Debal'tseve—
    marvelous produce.

*

      Incarnations worked the soil.

Live bullets dispersed the evening.
I ran to see the feathers.

The countryside strained;
    shrewd contradiction.

The sweet bitterness of myth.

The wild field was militant—
a weary undulation,
....torn by
..hot wind.

In the coalfield,
........rumor broke
........and stabbed.

*

I found death
............accurate.

I was struck
........that I was understood.

HAZEM FAHMY

THE BILLIONAIRE
(ARE YOU BOAT OR SUBMARINE?)

The answer is: neither. You are on land,
obviously,   your swimsuit unused

in well over a year. You felt the sand
           between your cold toes on a windy afternoon in early June

& called it a day. You got food alone
           because your friends had other places to be & your love

was hundreds of miles away. Because
           you were on land, you watched the ocean

like you would a dog in the park, admiring its capacity
           for cruelty from a safe distance. You did not

think of boats, but you did think of land   specifically
that which you do not own. You reject the myth

of your own temporary embarrassment   but at night
           you pray your name makes its way onto a home   nonetheless.

                              You like to think property has lost
                              its seductive hold on your throat

as you lie down in the room you rent for an amount that is comparably reason-
   able & eat your
Thai food, alone. You failed

statistics in high school, & miserably so   but you continue
to understand that everything is a matter of probability:

> the motorcycle that missed your foot by inches;
> your love coming back to New York,
>
> on a rainy day in the gloomiest of springs,
> the water becoming a safer bet than the land.

In the obits mourning the billionaires, it is mentioned that they paid
$250k to die before the eyes of the entire world

> a laughably cheap ticket
> compared to the cost of carrying

a child onto a floating grave. Whose mercy
would you rather stake your life on? The ocean's?

Or a European coast guard's? I know
what odds I'd take

> just as I know I am always hopelessly
> closer to being boat than submarine, more
>
> likely to flee land than risk never returning
> because of a hubris afforded by oil & old money & other
>
> crimes we will surely hear about in the coming months. I will

never be submarine, & so I pray the same is true
for the boat. I just want a room

to go home to after the beach & know my body to be whole & dry
& mine

& mine
& mine

ABIGAIL SWOBODA

IN BULK

Freedom is moving out of Stewartstown
       our little town can't handle any more
       building   but they are constantly planting
       new homes   potted strawberries   Chesapeake
       Bay Helicopters   & then the theft &
       the trash & the dog crap   Spray the garbage
       with cheap perfume to prevent rummaging
       rummage only when you are sure there is

no other way   FULL   MOON ALERT   God Bless
& hold your heads high   replace the cartridge
in the faucet   park   on the street instead
A manmade island   built by the village
something very close   to community
something special   about being chosen
Church bells are ringing   the sun is shining
We are the backbone   no one stands a chance

DOVER TASTES WORSE THAN DALLASTOWN

I think we need a system to soften
        water   to right our steel mailboxes turned
        totally around   to grind our dry stumps
        Infrastructure does not last forever
        could be worse   Could be Michigan   Paying
        more for contaminated water   the
        built-in pool & the playground & picnic
        area   kayaks   K-9s   & the South

Central Pennsylvan   ia Search & Rescue
team   According to   Psalm 139
our shoulders are broad   & we are laughing
it off   felting &   dyeing & weaving
& milking it off   Mark your calendars
we will be searching   again at 9   Please
please wear orange or red   look for her body
Amen   Amen   A   MEN   Amen   Amen

PAUL S UKRAINETS

PERSPECTIVE GRID

It is too early for the pavement to meet
the feet of commuters. A van, white,

with a stripe of undilutable bog green
across its body, sits at the curb of Prechistenka

& surveys the Moskva river. You'd expect
the sunlight to be a colder, more chromatic blue,

but it washes the river's surface in sunrise glows.
Scales of light bouncing from the clean ceramic

pavement into many windows: faces of stout
apartment buildings, punctuated by commas

of small kiosks, ellipses of traffic mirrors bending
corners. The thin smell of exhaust fumes already

begins to layer itself into the air. The van's windshield
fogged, the sky's painting of sun briefly trapped

in its coat. Two bodies in dark-blue uniforms,
with under-polished gold pins on their shoulders

& chests, lean against it. Smoke escapes their mouths
from Parliaments smothered between their red fingers.

The van's back windows are dark and crossed over
with bars, splitting the prisoners' view into a grid.

I have tried to write this poem many times.
There are about ten people in the van, one of them

a journalist. His camera rolls over the streets
of Moscow as the van loops around the city; once

they pull into the station, there's only 24 hours left
of arrest. The protesters in the van's stomach did not

prepare coats. In the frame I later see them shivering
on benches, one arm's hairs touching the other's.

They have spent the night's hours here & the *where*
of *where to go* is slipping away from them. Some lean

their jaws on the cold wall, their post-baton compress.
I don't know how this poem ends. A director cuts

the journalist's scene and places it bluntly
into the film. In a few minutes, the credits roll.

But the people in the van stay unnamed to me.
I came to the screen, to language, looking

to transform pain. But all each image taught me
was to just keep looking, since each epiphany

needs a frame. My eyes scan their surroundings
for a place to rest, or bury, the measurements

they extract, stumbling on, over it.

EMILY HOLLANDER

THE SCIENCE PODCAST BROS TELL ME WHAT LIFE IS

It is carbon-based and water-dependent, and it is all as far as we know genetic, and
this does not really answer my question.   The early earth was a late bombardment,
big hot and big heavy they don't call it the Hadean for nothing   it was a weak air pressing
differently on a body atmosphere volcanic and   there were no oceans yet because nothing
was quite solid.   There was a planet but there was no Earth until there was life, which

also does not answer my question.   Electrons were given freely and now they are taken, which

begins to answer my question. The boys say that viruses are not life because they are not self-
sustaining, and I'd like to know what exactly is "self-sustaining" because I am no longer sure I am
alive.   Any cell is a genetic jumping,   so I think life is a bit sluttier than they'd like
to admit, and if viruses are parasites of life,   I cannot imagine   a more model organism.

DAVID GREENSPAN

from GLITCH, MICHIGAN

Rhetorical like a father. If
body, then worm. If bullied,
then warm. Piss leak,
past and shake with hands. Fingers
grim, nail through other
lumber. If bile, than wane. Watery
rat tail between
dredge and gloat. The body,
then bodies, ratted and
watery. If body, then rivered,
reverbed, lumbered. No
bloat oar worm. You
ourselves leak father.

Inventory of individual of walls. Rude brick plays ball thrown against. Gray washed school you don't remember. Map with chalk. Recuperate north, east, south, west with never eat sour watermelon. More: not easy so what, now earn some wince.

Why Debord? Step on
garden implement to
farce, breath opposite,
wilt music. Debord
behind a clown
care. Goofishly unlarge,

yes small. "Sadness
a privilege," he theories over tire
pressure. Debord's desk
symmetrical with Wite-Out. He paints
teeth an oyster
unknown to the even
richest sturgeon.

Bright with I all
syllogism. Todays of
young, ready to smatter
applause then moth.
That's all. Money
mothers the toy. I
shellac, shallow, somehow,
shallot. Worms and rats
my closest. Place dogteeth on,
pebble what remains.

What garage? You unwanted as pennies in. Sweat while limestone, run once wheat. Chicken before evening's evening. School field day, dust in eyes, awards free handed. You're error of speech simple as fine linen. Suit, yes, but fraudulent leaves, meager something or mother, theft a rhubarb.

Grammar of *replace subject with predicate sometimes* to *achieve insurrectional dawning*. Correct posture toward *misery of out of the misery*. Debord sample Kierkegaard. You swap *detours, jam always returns pantry, you word which isn't which bothers the memory it awakens*.

I aspire to personhood, to
incisor chipped,
irritant. Glitch
improvised while perform
morning. I provisional,
sham at breakfast. Before

sun, fog taken at face
valve, frog in mouth, raise
temperature. Pace
spoon against upper
palette. Frog squeak, I
rebrand something closure to
nervous system.

Why does lunchmeat taste blood? Standard elementary. Imprecise light, field seeded, chalked margins, soccer goal before hallway. Headlong. Art class acrylic, shimmy and wave dry, no discernable figure. Not discreet rubber band stretched finger, gesture at face, mine face, alter face's crying, mine.

PALOMA YANNAKAKIS

RUNOFF ZONE

> *Su escultura se levantaba como*
> *un negativo en la ciudad*
> *…viaje sectorial inacabable.*
> —DIAMELA ELTIT, *El Padre mío*

Wonder that the piled stones don't fall,
abandoned cargo, signal

already destroyed, makeshift
cardboard

       tinder home

Fig 53a. The shore line of dispossession forms a contour line.
Suppose the water level of need rises 50cm above its original land. The contour
line, formed by the shore line, changes and takes a new shape,
       one-way arrow now joining all the points 50 cm higher than
the original lake level (Fig. 53b).

*Fig 53b. When the water level rises, a new contour line is formed. The water
level rises.*
bags of trash line the fringes, unrestored frontlines   a transparent umbrella
poster posing as home wall: a memorial of faces   walk on through

Contour lines are useful means to illustrate the topography of a field on a flat map; the height of each contour line is indicated on the map so that the hills and depressions can be identified.

Pulling cargo's all I got, two cinder blocks
                                             on a milk crate tied to a rope
city barnyard
underbrush knee deep with a few stacks of flesh
stuck with the stepped-over sticks sucking
it in no rest no for the rest
grace
                laid down with a few
                             aaahhandful of coins, some candles
                          the gentle wick melts

Fig 54. A three dimensional view
Such a [representation] [gives] a [very good idea] [of] what [the] field [looks like] in reality. Unfortunately, it requires much skill to draw.

from this vantage point behind the blank
skull a field of lack abundant   & drops
of wax to ease the wick   of clothed knees
riddled with-skill-pressingdown incens-
cent -enti- viiii
-zzed and doesn't it
_____ THE PRESENT _____ ACHE

3.4.3. Mistakes in the contour lines
Contour lines of different heights can never cross each other.

In the market: someone yells,
I'm a man! ain't I?
Can you give me something
to eat, just one fruit?

next to a statue must be
a historical figure
one hurries past

Fig 56. WRONG; crossing contour lines
A contour line is continuous; there can never be an isolated piece of contour line
somewhere on the image, as shown in Fig 57.

covertly converting the dented wind
breathing through
extreme weather, fluted through
didn't cross the sidewalk

                        singing or sighing I couldn't tell, wet collar
                          integument of a broken armature
                        singing kept along

                    peninsular pericardium
                    perforated at the hinge

and filled with trepidation
asked for a drenched cup
blade in teeth in this quiver of sun

          sometimes a river   anodine around you
          scale of longing

                    eradicated the jocular jaw   unduly wielded

on schedule

                  to be complete

clavicle choir mitred in the tongue and groove

fed birdfeet for food

hidden in derision's hide
sudden rapture piecemeal in
equanimous folds

a little lee way, no?
just the somber partition

fled field in crick of throat
& *through inner supplication*
avoid stiffened muscles (Weil)

reset the table
a padlocked apprehension

muddy tracks of ghostly splendor
    ventricle treacle

low railing of cement
beneath the lamplit leaves

Fig. 57. WRONG; an isolated piece of contour line
Crossing contour lines would mean that the intersection point has two different
elevations, which is impossible (see Fig. 56).

pity the open beak

to advance in all directions at once
until the strips of meat come down
from their hooks

                                        chirp of the unfinished meal

repleat

      crushed wheel

(it was to be of my own design
did not succeed past
the threshold of holes)

                                     Fig. 55. A two-dimensional view

                                     how one might stretch in sleep
                                     given enough room

                                     gravel burrowed
                                     into the breast

came upon
a small dead mouse sequestered
between two unevenly laid bricks

for certain a disenchanted star
when in danger make a husk
make like nothing

                                                pennies
                                              left on the ledge

                                                    blank ex-
                                                    penditure braying
                                                    with back turned

the puffy black coat he slips it off
from side to side slides it over his arms
in perfect syncopation pantomiming a wave
breakdancer on the station platform

It could have been a hallucination.
I wanted to look away but could not.

Question: What is the real distance between points A and B on the field when these two points are apart on a map whose scale is 1 to 2?

3.4.4. Scale of a map
To be complete and really useful, a map must have a defined scale.

This is the place in which we found ourselves. Crude iron,
a structure with no end and no beginning.

Fig. 58. Measuring the distance between A and B

the train pulls away   he pulls on
his coat the lunatic role   black trash bag bouncing on

FUTURE CONTINUOUS

We have your number and all quarters. Fortune folds us up—without a line to the dead, we can hear the blood rushing, a cup against our drum. The gifts we make ourselves (destiny or doom) hold up in flat daylight, some familiar oath, some new contract: we are finger-deep in the sand, spinning and spiny, no new lines but this soft, fat earth. Still falling off the page, we ziiiiiip. We hold the mirror slant—sky and her big feelings bounce. What can we mine of the future and if, oh not extraction, then what can we lift, whole and breathing, over our heads?

TALIA FOX

NOTES ON TIME TRAVEL
IN THE MATRILINEAL LINE

I   tools for transit

most beverages but especially milky sodas and peach coca cola; seawater; cups; certain fish and some fruit; most trains but especially loop trains, light rails, bullet trains, metros, and all other trains; a mistranslated text; grass

II   press   moon (*unlisted)

you stayed at the river too long ! in the spring before the summer stabbings. when you turned to journey home you found the sky filled by thousands of crane flies blocking your way with their shitty, drunken bodies bobbing in unison from that moment until the end of time

III   press   train (*must press without touching anything)

(In "Letter to a Man," Mikhail Baryshnikov slinks across a bare stage in a tuxedo while an image of the snow is projected behind him. As Polish ballerina Vaslav Nijinsky, Baryshnikov explains that, though he has never been a soldier, he understands what it is to be a soldier: "I have a powerful imagination.")

IV   please, be careful of your arms and legs

the image may be wrong—i didn't write enough down but in train cars I hear baryshnikov repeating the same line like a spell: "I am not Christ; I am Nijinsky."

V   press   seawater (*must press with the whole of the body)

(Chapter 11 of the Heikemonogatari recounts the decisive battle of the Genpei War, between the Taira and Minamoto clans: the Battle of Dan-no-Ura, a sea battle which left the water red with blood. Today the crabs in the area have shells which look to be inscribed with human faces.)

(or so they say, or so they say)

VI   press   moon (*unlisted) and   milky soda

the curse is simple, and it begins with water

 the water my mother bathed me in was crab water (it is, after all, the water alotted for soldiers and the children of soldiers and their children and especially their children)

like a spell, like a spell !

when i close my eyes i am wading through a shallow river at evening. i come across a forest clearing where bodies have been strung up, faceless, bobbing in the trees

INA CARIÑO

IT FEELS GOOD TO COOK RICE

        it feels good to cook rice
it feels heavy to cook rice
it feels familiar
        good
  & *heavy*   to cook rice

        when I cook rice
      it is because hunger is not just
          an emptiness

but a longing   for multo:
        the dead who no longer linger

      two fingers in water
      I know just when to stop:
      right under the second knuckle

in the morning   chew it
            with salted egg
in the evening   chew it
            with salted onion
at midnight   eat it
          slovenly
    with your peppered hands   licking
relishing   each cloudmorsel
            sucking greedy   as if

                there will no longer be any such thing
as rice

            good
is not the idea of pleasure
                rather
                    it is the way
                          I once tripped
                    spilled a basket
of hulls & stones onto soil —
homely sprinkle of husks
as if for a sending off —
              how right it was: palms
              brushing the chalk of it
              swirls rising in streaking sun

            heavy
is not the same as burden
                  rather it is falling rice
                        as ghostly footfalls —
              trickling mounds
                        scattered on wood —
my dead lolo in compression socks
my dead lola in red slippers scuffing
& a slew of yesterday's titos & titas
              their voices traveling to me
              tinny   ringing
              as if from yesterday's nova

familiar just
        what it sounds like
family
        blood
home
        marrow

bone
   grit
calcified memories
      of things that feel good
          & heavy
   calcified
     as in made stronger by mountain sun
   only to have them crumble
     after enough time has passed
   (just like the mountain forgot what it used to be)

     still
it feels good to cook rice
it feels good to eat rice even by myself
& it feels familiar to know
   with each grain I swallow
I strap myself to my own
       heavy
     hunger

ROSA ALCALÁ

YOU TO THE FUTURE

What would you have said to the future? Future, you will have no scientist in it. Future, your scientist was kissing a Canadian. Future, you could have told me, "Don't go to his apartment, depress the doorbell for many seconds, wait in his favorite diner around the corner, call him from the dark and humid underground of your last rumbling hope." But, Future, let me tell you something truly remarkable: there were payphones on subway platforms, which was great when you needed one, but if you needed one, things were often not so great. You were late for an interview, or you wanted to be told, "Don't get on that train. I love you. Come back to bed." No one on a subway payphone wanted to hear, "Hold on." You were lost, trying to buy weed, calling some guy's beeper. The receiver and keypad were archives of body-cum-city, and in these moments of disorientation, of numbers black and waxy and sticky, the pointer finger brought you closer to your desire with its impeccable memory. You needn't be told, lovers will misfire feelings wherever and whatever the mode, but in you, Future, no one will know what it's like to make a collect call, to reverse the charges. Nor remember the ode a Spanish poet wrote to his light bulb late one night in the kitchen.

GERAMEE HENSLEY

DEARLY BELOVED
(A PREFATORY QUADRAPHONICS)

1.

The plasticity of knowledge is why I'm still here. Saeed Jones: "But I run past what I thought was the end of myself" i.e. loogied over the borderline, the pinto of being spit out lacquers me. How else to exit a mouth—saying what exactly? After imperialism splits lives like chaff and seed, we must leave our mothers. When belonging turns to out to be longing, all joy goes hollow, and a dry laughter becomes our only name. Now we live in a far-off memory bound by sound and threaded into living time.

it is no bitterness we inhabit, but a past, what's left, sharp

as grief, is our true fatherland. i run past all there ever was.

2.

The plasticity of knowledge is why I'm still here. Audre Lorde: "Sometimes, bitterness were a whetstone, I could've sharpened its striking edges on its hide or tongue" i.e. in lyric, I can exist sharp / but once it pierces a song, it can rip truth in pieces. How its edges can carry a self / it floral decay, I presume it would only last us, as is sorrow in gripping my pain belongs to speak. To make sorrow doesn't weary its mother tongue.

make no mistake, our native tongue was the end

of bitterness. if language were all there ever was, i run past no nation, but a grief we inhabit, a whetstone, or maybe the end of fatherland.

3.

The plasticity of knowledge is why I'm still here. Xenmas: "I'm what's left or maybe I'm all there ever was" i.e. for the jacket with loops on its arm, I bought a filipino flag patch, planted it, then flaunted it to Ma. When asked what should go underneath, she smiled and said, "the american flag." The Philippine republic grants citizenship jus sanguinis. Blood or dirt says we are people. But who says mercy then slips it between our shut eyes? Mortar: to mend. Mortar: to bombard. Mortar: what withstands the crushing pestle.

i could be what's left. the end of myself, it is no nation, but a sharp was.

4.

The plasticity of knowledge is why I'm still here. Enit Crioxn: "It is no nation on it is" i.e. language & a tongue inhabit, but a mistake. Make no mistake, it was myself. But a nation is our tongue belonged. To land it into a mix of mother, to muster mind, bitter, matter, moss, muster. To mother, muster a moss, matter of myth. To mercy myself a mystery & mystic.

DOUGLAS KEARNEY

TEEF

What I realize when looking at you I wist there: us is a splitting of certain shadows and in saying splitting what they think of but portioning schisming or headaches at figuring a figure out with our nonstop arithmetic thing. You all Don't go thinking of them my bad my same old same old and see I see you yeah y'all said that Don't while smiling which eased me so your teeth—by looks too—seem like pills but since you are smiling and I see them all rowed you ain't swallowed them—the pills that're teeth they chime together still that's a figure. I figure if I could have done anything ere maybe I could have swallowed that other them we aren't to think on and left no nothing for y'all to get as ill—when I'd go correctly so before y'all perhaps I wouldn't have spit none of them out even. But now you stopped smiling so have I and y'all all: For real tho stop thinking bout them—I'm sorry they take so much of my mind—I'm sorry. I start instead a story of a speculative physics—so it don't begin Once upon a time no no no it goes What has to happen was and in this story shadow don't see light as what must happen for praxis. At this your lips part some like a smile soon come back only now no no so many of your teeth missing. No

What has to happen was...

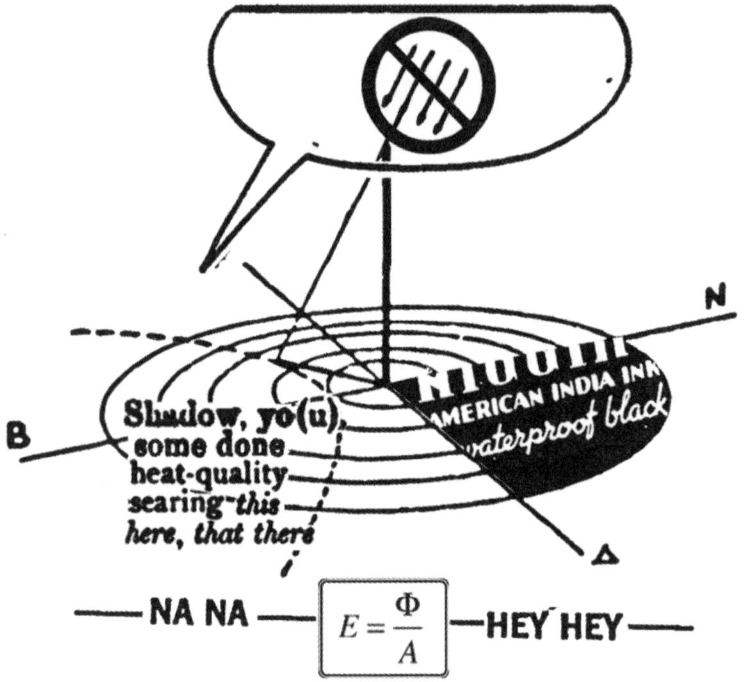
N
B
Shadow, yo(u)
some done
heat-quality
searing this
here, that there
AMERICAN INDIA INK
waterproof black
NA NA
$E = \frac{\Phi}{A}$
HEY HEY

tic
tic
tic
tic
tic
 tic
  tic
SHADOW
   tic

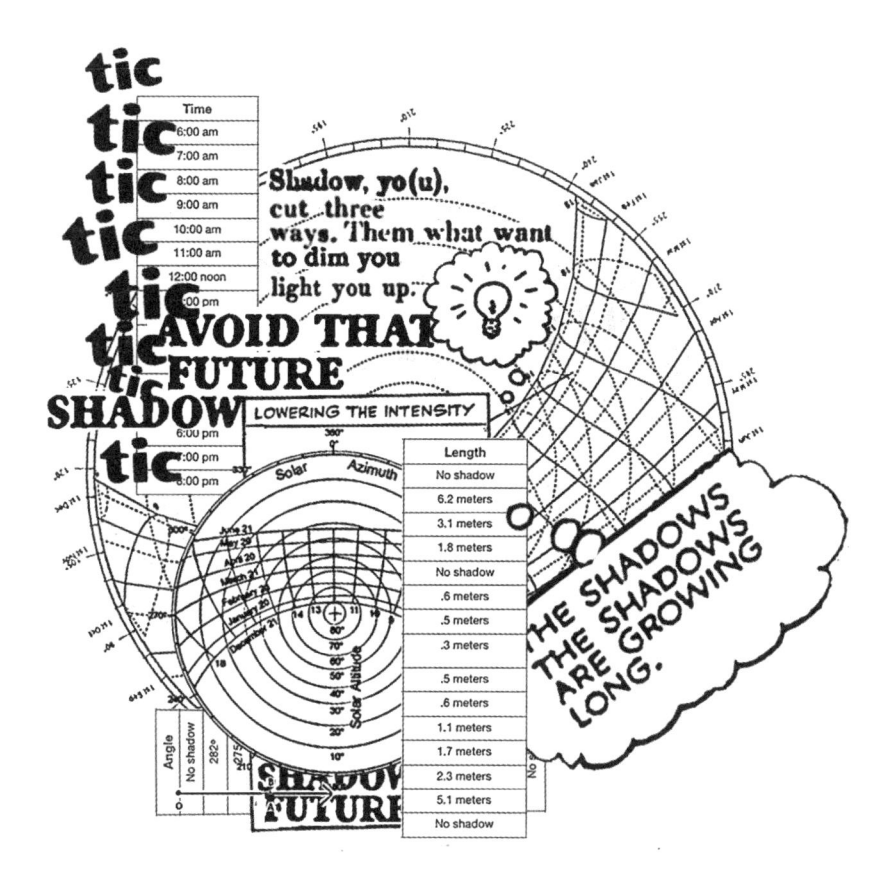

Shadow, yo(u), cut three ways. Them what want to dim you light you up.

AVOID THAT FUTURE

LOWERING THE INTENSITY

SHADOW FUTURE

THE SHADOWS
THE SHADOWS
ARE GROWING
LONG.

Time	
6:00 am	
7:00 am	
8:00 am	
9:00 am	
10:00 am	
11:00 am	
12:00 noon	
1:00 pm	
2:00 pm	
3:00 pm	
4:00 pm	
5:00 pm	
6:00 pm	
7:00 pm	
8:00 pm	

Length
No shadow
6.2 meters
3.1 meters
1.8 meters
No shadow
.6 meters
.5 meters
.3 meters
.5 meters
.6 meters
1.1 meters
1.7 meters
2.3 meters
5.1 meters
No shadow

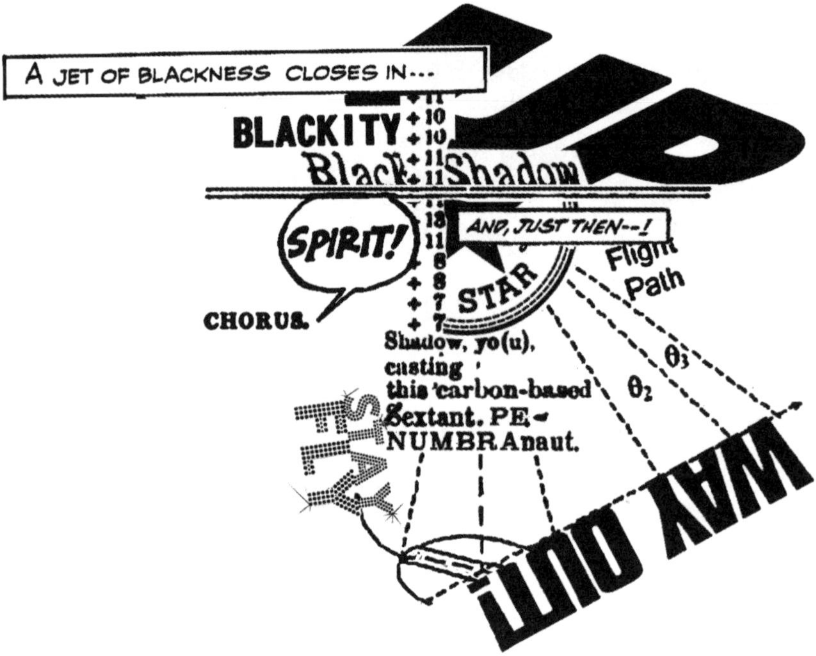
A JET OF BLACKNESS CLOSES IN...
BLACKITY
Black Shadow
SPIRIT!
CHORUS.
AND, JUST THEN--!
STAR
Flight Path
θ3
θ2
Shadow, yo(u), casting this 'carbon-based Sextant. PE-NUMBRAnaut.
STAY
FLY
WAY OUT!

afro
PRIMARY COIL
+12V
SECONDARY COIL
WITH DOUBLE HEAD.
VERY WELL THEN. I SHALL DEMONSTRATE THE USES OF THE ELECTRO-WEAVE.
Shadow, yo(u), Shangó axes controller. I mean work. The roots.
YES, I.
Ultra
X
MY UNCONQUERABLE HAIR!

SOON THE TRANSFORMER WAS READY...

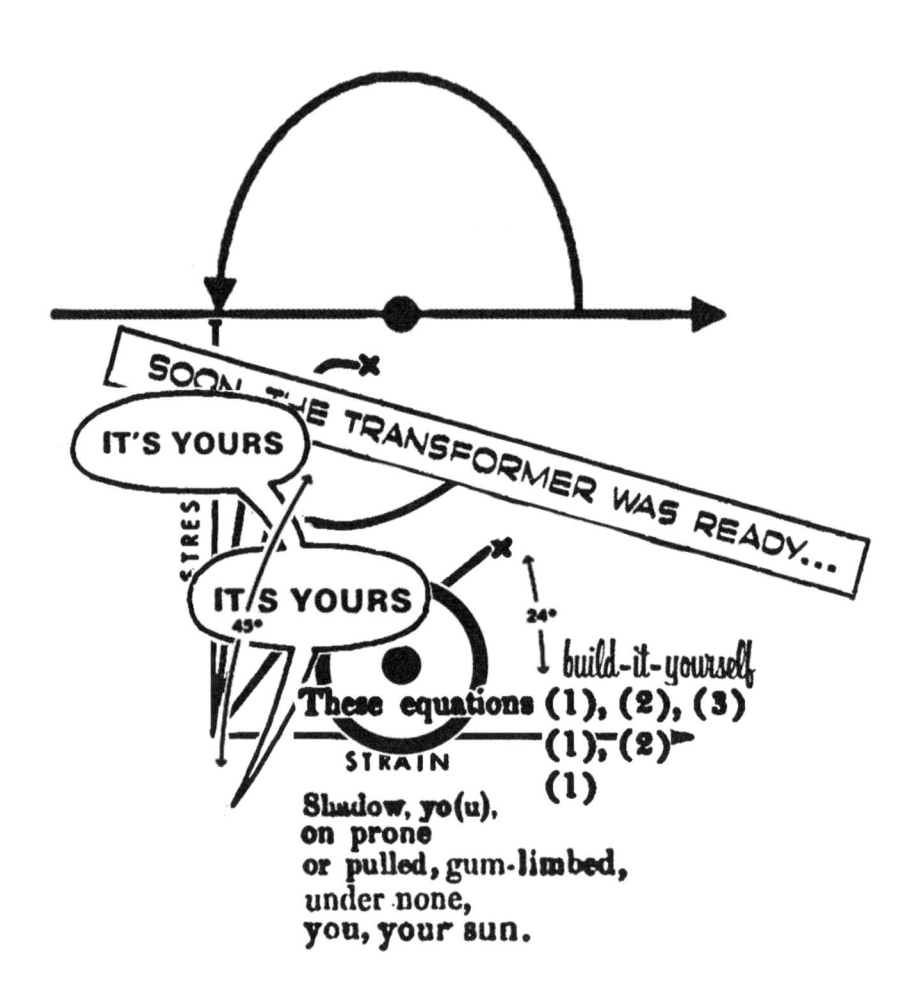

IT'S YOURS

IT'S YOURS

build-it-yourself

These equations (1), (2), (3)
(1), (2)
(1)

Shadow, yo(u),
on prone
or pulled, gum-limbed,
under none,
you, your sun.

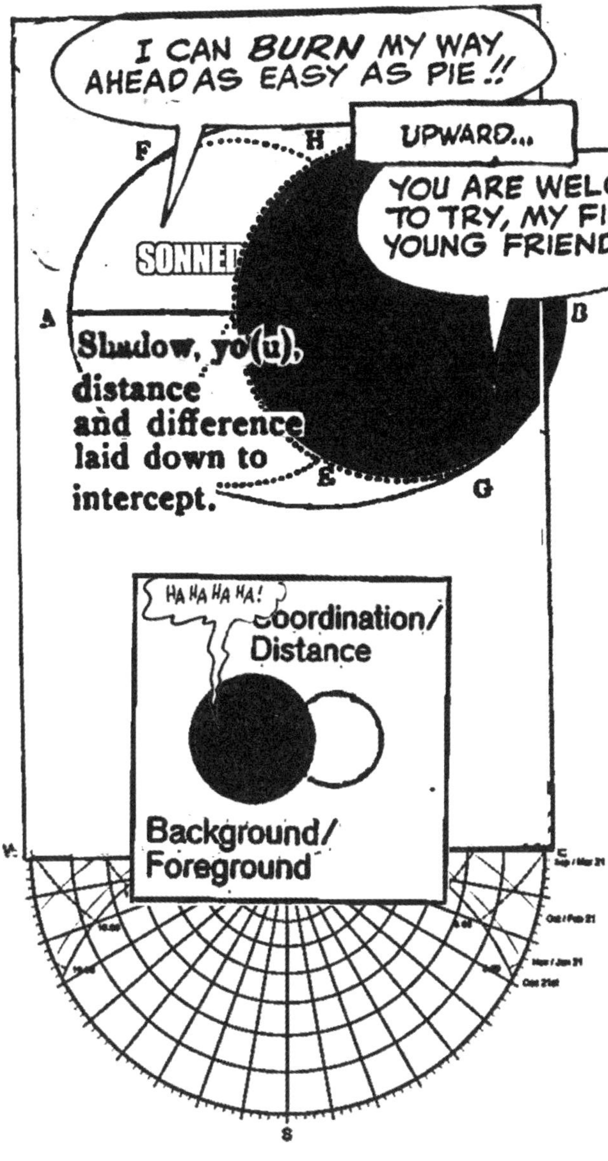
I CAN BURN MY WAY AHEAD AS EASY AS PIE!!
UPWARD...
YOU ARE WELCOME TO TRY, MY FIERY YOUNG FRIEND!
SONNED
Shadow, yo(u), distance and difference laid down to intercept.
HA HA HA HA!
Coordination/ Distance
Background/ Foreground

MYLO LAM

TRI NHAN 004 WITNESSES & SONNETIZES A STARLING MURMURATION

all it takes is one of you to break from the perch
your flock will follow   millions cawing
you will not be banished from us!
even if that banishment was your own doing
   (((((((we will be your echoes!)))))))

nowhere to escape to   weave into
fleeting dead space
faith our nearest sisters & brothers
don't & won't kill us
   (((((((& us them)))))))

heartbeat upon your heartbeat upon my heartbeat
rhythming into a howling feather drum
we begin we forget we go on
forging in our forgetfulness   bebop temples

one starling   shadows away   a ghost among the millions
an omen   someone has died   somewhere nearby
   (((((where the flock cannot yet follow)))))

GERÓNIMO SARMIENTO CRUZ

from WHALEFALL

     of those assembled here
         our banalities
     this concerns whatever we
    are saprotrophic
     nuestras pieles
   dicen casi todo
    a glitch exceeding
   its duration
    the cadence
  of its materials
striving for smallness
    feral
   driftless in our orbit
      pero hay silencios también
     vocablos foráneos
      e indómitos
       you choose your face
    &prerogative
   we'll craft the mask
     &head seaward
      pero te tropiezas con el diptongo
    i'll pause here now
   because of time
  eres mi yunta
  es pregunta
    how many fingers you got left
   stairs are an easy

        language to learn
            the comfort
                of the postapocalyptic
                    posibilidades
                        amorfas todavía
                  without outsides we're
                          nounless &perfectlyfine
                        noster mandibular branch
                for stridulation
                      for babble
    a sense of the delicately discreet
            has never accompanied us
                      preciousnesses
                  long imported
                        we ignore dispensability
                dedicated to water&flux
              our metaphor
                    for metaphor
                &fruiting bodies
      just new to the new moon
ad hominem undertow
      suck you into you &i
  solute the lips
xolo&growl
      extraparliamentary
          escuincle hirsuto
              y ladrabar
        been revenue
            into the solvent's
          exhalations
     in gravitas
     dime cuándo tú
            amateur formlessness
                dime cuándo tú
                typed topos
              from afar
            vas a volver

                    percussor throughout
                        feitiço songs
                                    from across our
                            once is always is punctual
                                siempre de y espacio
                                orquidácea perenne
                                never did
                            manage
                                    to turn obsolescence
                                        on its head
                                pernoctar es
                    de mis verbos
                            predilectos
                        pero te lo presto
        there are
                numberless
                    ways to fall
                    so fall
        so injudiciously
                        orgulloso de mi
                arritmia
                        veo
                    la muerte bailando
                                    mis pasos
                            arrhythmia
                        she was
                            baptized
                    arrhythmia
                                de l'ouverture
                                        incorpóreos
                                    incorpóreas no
                                        puedo con éstas
                                night fell&
                                        every
                                    celestial
                        body appeared
                    to be rising

                                            137

                    sternenfall
                            language gallops
                        us
                    back to
                your patio
                    space
                        &time regardless
                    y qué
                si sí
                    chingadamadre
                        qué si la distancia
                es chantaje
                    perfunctory
                to the very least
        otherwise we'd be
            then by now
                    nómadas nos
        seguimos yendo
            y ya
ni
    cazamos
                sólo huímos
        find us
            on even
        ground
                this time
                    we'll teach our grammar
                            a veces
            caemos grande y a
veces ni
    molestamos
        al aire
            alveolar fati
                    guess you expect
                me to talk
                    about walls

138

why stand on the shoulders
                when you can
        lick their faces
                algo que acá
            nunca supimos
        fue qué le pasó
                a sam cooke
                        there's a line of words
                            like true
                                    just&brave
                                but also elvis
                        lo cuál no es
                            necesariamente malo
                a pesar de que lo es
                    how far am i from canaan
                    how far am i from aztlán
            aún así me
                como nopales
            con gusto
                    inclusive víboras
                            we don't
                                fall quite
                        the same you
                    and we and the
                clatter we
                    although
                altogether
                    are
        motilidad
                morena
                    solfege
                        this not
            sin exhibir el precio
        solo los años que
                enuncian
                    vida vivida
                when i say

              you
                    hardly do i ever
                          mean to imply
                  that there is
                an i around
       ésta es tu frontera
                tidal dance to
           squanto beat
tuya la manufactura
      tuya la manutención
           if it is
                to go ahead
           it is to stop
                suyas las manos
              lest asphyxia
   lest scansion
           cercenadas
                desde estas hendiduras
                      you limp your
                          pontiff self down
                patuxet ghosts now
                                pines fifty miles out then
           que la marea inundará
          this bruise of
                   my underside
                            me lees la llaneza
                del mar
                en sus bordes
                we don't
             remember akin
        fetisso in the currency
                          sin lluvia ni adverbios
   go breath a tongue for both
                        en estas aguas no nadas
      hoofing endlessness&
             abhored
         but not absolved

                              desaparecémonos debajo
         come the rarefied moment
                         you should know
                                      no more
                            than one or
                two abstractions
         three at most or
                    tal vez las barcas
                          resistirán
                   y estos órganos
                                filiformes
                       se sabrán
                                   transatlánticos
                                      the latter
                                  sheer summerings
                         do you feel ill
                             feelest thou illest
                                      de telares
                          acéfalos muere
                                    el pescado por la proa
                                     you think i should
                            talk about walls
                       que las barcas
                   siempre hundidas
                          rehúsan alterar
                      su rumbo
                             that it'd be
                                   alright to hate this
                       self as long
                  as there is love for
                       your mores
                                &clinamen
                   por el que llegaron
          tanto escandinavo
                      como cúrcuma
                   our embrace
                       we've let down

LORRAINE RICE

AFFIDAVIT OF LOSS

I, citizen of a contradiction, hereby affirm that this confluence of matter and reason is truer than any river weaving the green and fallow of ages expired, assured.

I, daughter of havoc, having been duly sworn to collect and keep the memories in accordance with ghosts, hereby attest that:

    1. I am an heir of the body of the mother with shared initials and an affinity for water. As such, I was issued a place on the land north of Mill Swamp, including the swamp, a moss cradle in the cypress knees and roots.

2. On a Monday in November under a waning gibbous I discovered that my birthright, which contained valuable items like Safe and Home, was lost before my first cry shred the night.

3. Frayed strands of the loss include the following:
    a. I have reported the loss to the stars and await their reply; sent missives in cobalt bottles sailing on the tide; commiserated with mourning doves in hopes my grief might fly.
    b. The last known location is the seed of destruction deep in the father's belly. Other prospects include her hollowed-throat displacement; the blood-thick cord.

4. I further attest that I am reconciled with the irretrievable. More than the land I desire to decipher the path of the land from one false claim of possession to the next. I seek the story in its entirety, so the ghosts can rest with ease elusive

in life. Name the weight of sanctioned thievery from clay to bone. Loosen the knot before the blue moon wanes.

5. I am executing this affidavit to attest to the excision of vital notes from the family song, a missing verse that accounts for the failed rhythm; to secure another birthright while this earth-bound body holds me. An inheritance for my children less rotted root, more gold-flecked sky.

_____

(AFFIANT NAME)

_____

(AFFIANT SIGNATURE)

P.C. VERRONE

ARC-HIVE

We – are – all – in – this – belly – together – wriggling – through – these – cata – combs – as – turbulent – waters – beat – against – our – capsule –   Workers – of – individual – unknowingly – in – ter – sect –ing – paths – lapping – nectar – into – waxy – conjectures –   Outside – the – monsoon – rages – on –   Inside – we – nest – le – our – pollen – pocked – bodies – against – our – honied – histories – while – the – other – beasts – cry – out – to – their – pagan – gods –   Time – is – short –   With – only – enough – to – feed – our – jelly – citations – to – dreams – of – rain – bowed – futures – we – cannot – take – even – a – moment – to – ask – if – our – God – knows – that – two – cannot – steer – this – ship – and – exhume – these – bodies –   Should – the – Flood – ever – find – inadequacy – in – the – hardened – labor – of – our – tongues – certain – and – instant – death –   In – the – hexagonal – dark – we – are – taught – to – miss – the – hum – of – our – fellow – workers – and – forget – the – touch – of – their – fur – Until – we – remember – that – finding – the – Garden – in – this – Down – Pour – is – only – the – most – myopic – piece – of – it –   Then – put – down – the – pencil – and – pocket – the – tape – recorder – come – to – the – bleeding – circle – and – dance –

ENCORE & ON A LOOP

opens with an invitation, breathe it in and let it out, the instrumental near the album's end, a one-way ticket, a window seat, the sound they make you fall in love with, track 2, observation train, whole lives in the blurry distance, the collapse of time, everyone's got a swimming pool nobody uses, the singer sings to slow the syllables of e-ve-ry beautiful thing we can see, the mountains unmoving, so say it, the thing you haven't said, debt, dad, death, the soaring bridge, when we were 22 everything was possible, our small and inconsequential lives, less temperance, no nostalgia, try to say their name when you say you love them, delete the photo, all those people you've left, the mountains now moving, in unison, vocals in harmony, the cover better than the original, remember the ceiling you wake up to, raw nerve, permanent scar, to abandon versus to leave, neighborhoods fade, nature bends, why didn't you visit when you had the chance, how did you go on with the weight of it all, so much held in the three letters of etc., I want to bathe in milk, eat bread, listen solely to the soundtrack to our lives, watch the movies of our dreams, on repeat, all that pining and planning, so little doing, song after song, let's hear it again, one more time

ON THERAPY

say yes when anyone asks, it can happen all of a sudden, without the writing on the wall, some proof that the person is yearning, clawing for language, craving clarity, with grace, with gratitude, over time, as a gift and not an exchange, therapy not as a luxury but as a practice, health breeds health, daily, glacial pace, ill-equipped, incremental dissolution, uncanny estrangement, mirroring, Maya says that all we have is time and we can only control how we make use of it, our time, our pleasure, this civilization is sunsetting, discover, recover, team or family, at sunrise, it's easier to go, it's easier to go it alone, the two-body problem, the new lover's arms, the fragments, the pages without dates, you call everything you don't want to think about a distraction, because love itself and the models of it have failed, to walk away, to live without revision, to fix your own problems, to be unburdened by regret, the films are filled with the romance of heartbreak, a shock to the system, the dread of untangling your own logic, in boxes, in books, in rhetoric, your tics recorded in the pauses, your face refracted in the silverware, who keeps what and why, who knows to accept help, finding (yourself in) what you've written, the relationship has an end—one that doesn't feel like one

LENA KASSICIEH

AYAM ZAMAN

Our connection to our land, our heritage, our identities persists; we are Palestine
Lena Kassicieh

CONTRIBUTOR BIOS

ROSA ALCALÁ is the award-winning author of four poetry collections, most recently *YOU*, published in 2024. She is a translator of Latin American women poets, among them Cecilia Vicuña.

ESTHER G. BELIN is the author of two collections of poetry: *Of Cartography*, and *From the Belly of My Beauty*, and co-editor of *The Diné Reader*, teaches Native American Studies at Fort Lewis College and faculty in IAIA's MFA program.

LILLIAN-YVONNE BERTRAM is an African American writer, poet, artist, and educator. They are the author of *A Black Story May Contain Sensitive Content, Negative Money, Travesty Generator*, among others.

MAHOGANY L. BROWNE is a writer, playwright, organizer, & educator. She is the inaugural poet-in-residence at Lincoln Center and is working on her first adult fiction and fourth YA novel-in-verse. She lives in Brooklyn, NY.

SASHA BURSHTEYN is a poet. Her writing appears in *The Yale Review, The Paris Review Daily, Copper Nickel*, and elsewhere.

INA CARIÑO is a 2022 Whiting Award winner for poetry. They are the winner of the 2021 Alice James Award for *Feast*, published in March 2023.

MELISA CASUMBAL-SALAZAR has received support from *VONA, Kenyon Review, PAWA*, & *Minnesota Northwoods*. Her poetry is published or forthcoming in *Epiphany, Kaleidoscoped* & *Hot Pink*.

JADE CHO is a poet and educator. She splits her time between Oakland and Sacramento, where she lives with her partner and two elderly chickens.

MORIANA DELGADO is a writer from Mexico City. She graduated from the Iowa Writers' Workshop. *Peces de pelea* (Libros UNAM, 2022) is her first collection.

JACLYN DESFORGES is the author of a poetry collection, *Danger Flower* (Anstruther Books, 2021) and a picture book, *Why Are You So Quiet?* (Annick Press, 2020).

EM DIAL is a queer, Black, Taiwanese, Japanese, and white poet living in Toronto. They are the author of *In the Key of Decay*.

CAROLINA EBEID is a multimedia poet and author of *You Ask Me to Talk about the Interior* and the chapbook *Dauerwunder*. She is the current Bonderman Assistant Professor of Poetry at Brown University.

SAFIA ELHILLO is Sudanese by way of Washington, DC. She is the author of *The January Children*, *Girls That Never Die*, and the novels in verse *Home Is Not a Country* and *Bright Red Fruit*. She co-edited the anthology *Halal If You Hear Me* with Fatimah Asghar.

HAZEM FAHMY is a writer and critic from Cairo. His latest chapbook, *At the Gates*, was published in 2023 as part of Akashik Books' New-Generation African Poets series.

TALIA FOX is a poet based in San Francisco. She is a current MFA candidate in writing at Bard College.

STEFANIA GOMEZ received her MFA in poetry at Washington University in St. Louis. Her manuscript, *REDWORK*, is a finalist for the 2023 National Poetry Series. She is a finalist for the 2024 Ruth Lilly and Dorothy Sargent Rosenberg Poetry Fellowship

JAN-HENRY GRAY is the author of *Documents* (BOA Editions) and the chapbook *Selected Emails*. Born in the Philippines and raised in California, he teaches at Adelphi University in New York.

DAVID GREENSPAN is the author of *One Person Holds So Much Silence* (Driftwood Press) and the chapbook *Nervous System with Dramamine* (The Offending Adam).

MAX GREGG's poetic work intervenes in medical and institutional archives, in service of a queer and trans otherwise. They are a Henry Hoyns Fellow in Poetry at the University of Virginia.

JALYNN HARRIS is a writer, educator, & book designer from Baltimore. Her work can be found in Poets.org, *The Best American Poetry* 2022, & *Feminist Studies*.

A writer from Ohio, GERAMEE HENSLEY is Social Media Manager for *The Kenyon Review* and Poetry Editor at *Tinderbox Poetry Journal*. You can find them at geramee.com.

EMILY HOLLANDER hails from the cities and forests of the northeast where she hunts hidden poems, (re)writing toward a queer, nonlinear poetics. They are a current MFA candidate in poetry at Columbia University.

LENA KASSICIEH is a Palestinian-American anthropologist and multidisciplinary artist, interested in history and diaspora communities, anthropology, and memory. Lena is passionate about the power of objects, photographs, and archival materials.

DOUGLAS KEARNEY has published eight books ranging from poetry to essays. He is a Professor of English at the University of Minnesota–Twin Cities.

By constantly shifting between genres and mediums, SJ KIM-RYU's work generates an energy of the primordial, deeply rooted in improvisation, chaos, and rituals.

MYLO LAM and his family are refugees from Cambodia. His work has been published in *The Margins*, *Guesthouse*, *Palette Poetry*, *Quarterly West*, and *Beloit Poetry Journal*.

KATHARINA LUDWIG is a poet, writer, researcher and artist. Her/their work is concerned with narrative holes and the insurrectionary poetics of the 'wounded text.'

LUCIAN MATTISON is a US-Argentinian poet and translator. His third collection of poetry is *Curare* (C&R Press; 2023 International Latino Book Award Finalist).

CARI MUÑOZ is a queer poet and letterpress artist born and raised in Los Angeles. They received their M.F.A. from Arizona State University.

LORRAINE RICE is a writer and educator in Philadelphia. She mines memory and interrogates history to explore themes of identity and agency in her work.

GABRIEL RIDOUT is a Filipinx-American poet-scholar, currently a PhD student in English and American Literature at Washington University in St. Louis.

GERÓNIMO SARMIENTO CRUZ is a scholar, translator, and poet born in Mexico City and currently residing in Lexington, KY, on the occupied lands of the Shawnee, Cherokee, Chickasaw, and Osage people.

BRENDA SHAUGHNESSY, an Okinawan-Irish American poet, has authored seven collections, including *Tanya* (2023). Recipient of numerous fellowships, she co-created the opera "Sensorium Ex."

ABIGAIL SWOBODA is from Pennsylvania.

MAKSHYA TOLBERT lives in Charlottesville, VA, where they attend to poetry, pottery, and shade trees, at the meandering pace of Black ecological attention and aliveness. *Shade is a place* is her first book.

PAUL S UKRAINETS is a poet, translator, and recent MFA graduate from the Michener Center.

P.C. VERRONE'S plays have been showcased on Off-Broadway and regional stages and published by Playscripts. His fiction has appeared in the *Bridport Prize Anthology*, *FIYAH Magazine*, and *Elemental Forces* anthology.

LILLIE WALSH is a multidisciplinary research artist and bookmaker living in Seattle. She makes work as a means of renegotiating embodied experiences of history.

CHAUN WEBSTER is the author of *Wail Song: Wading in the Water at the End of the World* and *GeNtry!fication: Or the Scene of the Crime*, winner of the 2019 Minnesota Book Award for Poetry. He lives in Minneapolis.

KATHY WU (she/they) is an artist, writer, and educator. Through textiles, image, and data, she writes about scientific epistemology and extraction.

PALOMA YANNAKAKIS is a poet and teacher living in New York. You can find her work in *Lana Turner*, *Denver Quarterly*, and *Afternoon Visitor*.

EDITOR BIO

Naima Yael Tokunow is a writer, educator, artist, and editor living in New Mexico. Her work focuses on exploring Black queer femme identity, kinship, and futurity. She is the author of three chapbooks: *MAKE WITNESS* (2016); *Planetary Bodies* (2019); and *Shadow Black,* selected by Pulitzer Prize winner Jericho Brown for the Frontier Digital Chapbook Prize in 2020. Alongside her work as Nightboat's inaugural Editorial Fellow, she edits for Tupelo Press. She is blessed to be Black and alive.

ACKNOWLEDGMENTS

A huge and eternal thank you to the Nightboat team (Stephen Motika, Lindsey Boldt, Jaye Elizabeth Elijah, Gia Gonzales, Trisha Low, Santiago Valencia, Kit Schluter, Lina Bergamini, Emily Bark Brown, Dante Silva, and Kazim Ali) for their support, time, care, and thought partnership. Special gratitude to Santi for their deep partnership and cocreation on this project—your skills and wisdom have been a gift to me and to the work of this book! Without the team and Nightboat's Editorial Fellowship, this incredible collection would not exist in the world in the way it does.

Nothing but gratitude and adoration to Miles, Bayard, and Zora, whose support, joy, and love have shifted me in a million imperceptible ways. Miles, your labor and care with our kids made space for the forming of this book possible!

Gratitude to the displaced, oppressed, and otherwise marginalized peoples of this world (from Gaza to Congo, from Detroit to Sudan). This book is for and by and with you.

ABOUT NIGHTBOAT BOOKS

NIGHTBOAT BOOKS, a nonprofit organization, seeks to develop audiences for writers whose work resists convention and transcends boundaries. We publish books rich with poignancy, intelligence, and risk. Please visit nightboat.org to learn about our titles and how you can support our future publications.

The following individuals have supported the publication of this book. We thank them for their generosity and commitment to the mission of Nightboat Books:

Kazim Ali, Anonymous (5), Ava Avnisan, Jean C. Ballantyne, Bill Bruns, V. Shannon Clyne, The Estate of Ulla Dydo, Photios Giovanis, Amanda Greenberger, David Groff, Parag Rajendra Khandhar, Vandana Khanna, Shari Leinwand, Johanna Li, Elizabeth Madans, Martha Melvoin, Care Motika, Elizabeth Motika, The Leslie Scalapino – O Books Fund, Amy Scholder, Thomas Shardlow, Ira Silverberg, Benjamin Taylor, Jerrie Whitfield and Richard Motika, and Issam Zineh

This book is made possible, in part, by grants from the New York City Department of Cultural Affairs in partnership with the City Council and the New York State Council on the Arts Literature Program.